Test-Driven Development with React and TypeScript

Building Maintainable React Applications

Second Edition

Juntao Qiu

Apress®

Test-Driven Development with React and TypeScript: Building
Maintainable React Applications

Juntao Qiu
Wantirna, 3152, VIC, Australia

ISBN-13 (pbk): 978-1-4842-9647-9   ISBN-13 (electronic): 978-1-4842-9648-6
https://doi.org/10.1007/978-1-4842-9648-6

Managing Director, Apress Media LLC: Welmoed Spahr
Acquisitions Editor: Divya Modi
Development Editor: James Markham
Coordinating Editor: Divya Modi

Cover designed by eStudioCalamar

Cover image by Pixabay

Distributed to the book trade worldwide by Springer Science+Business Media New York, 1 New York Plaza, Suite 4600, New York, NY 10004-1562, USA. Phone 1-800-SPRINGER, fax (201) 348-4505, e-mail orders-ny@springer-sbm.com, or visit www.springeronline.com. Apress Media, LLC is a California LLC and the sole member (owner) is Springer Science + Business Media Finance Inc (SSBM Finance Inc). SSBM Finance Inc is a **Delaware** corporation.

For information on translations, please e-mail booktranslations@springernature.com; for reprint, paperback, or audio rights, please e-mail bookpermissions@springernature.com.

Apress titles may be purchased in bulk for academic, corporate, or promotional use. eBook versions and licenses are also available for most titles. For more information, reference our Print and eBook Bulk Sales web page at http://www.apress.com/bulk-sales.

Any source code or other supplementary material referenced by the author in this book is available to readers on GitHub (github.com/apress). For more detailed information, please visit http://www.apress.com/source-code.

Paper in this product is recyclable

To Mansi and Luna.

Table of Contents

About the Author xiii

About the Technical Reviewers xv

Acknowledgments xvii

Foreword 1 xix

Foreword 2 xxi

Introduction xxiii

Chapter 1: A Brief History of Test-Driven Development 1

What Is Test-Driven Development? 1

   The Red-Green-Refactor Cycle 2

   A Closer Look at Red-Green-Refactor 4

   Types of TDD 5

   Prerequisites of TDD 8

Other Techniques That Can Help Implement TDD 10

   Tasking 10

Summary 12

Further Reading 12

Chapter 2: Get Started with Jest 15

Set Up the Environment 15

   Install and Configure Jest 16

Jest at First Glance 18

   Basic Concepts in Jest 21

Using Matchers in Jest 25

　Basic Usages 25

　Matchers for Array and Object..27

　The Powerful Function expect 28

　Build Your Matchers..31

Mocking and Stubbing 34

　jest.fn for Spying 35

　Mock Implementation..35

　Stub a Remote Service Call 36

Summary...37

Chapter 3: Refactoring Essentials: The Basics You Need to Know 39

The Ten Most Common Refactorings 39

Let's Talk the Problem – Code Smells..40

　Long Files 40

　Big Props List 41

　Mixing Computation with Views 42

　Overuse of Mocks..43

　Not Following Established Principles 44

The Problem – ROT13 45

The Initial Implementation 45

The Top Ten Refactorings 47

　Step 1: Slide Statements 48

　Step 2: Extract Constant 49

　Step 3: Extract Function 50

　Step 4: Rename Parameter...51

　Step 5: Rename Variable...52

　Step 6: Extract Function 53

Step 7: Replace if-else with ? 55

Step 8: Extract Function 56

Step 9: Extract Parameter 57

Step 10: Extract Constant 58

Step 11: Slide Statements 59

Step 12: Move Fields 60

Step 13: Function to Arrow Function 61

Step 14: Simplify Logic 62

Summary 63

Chapter 4: Test-Driven Development Essentials 65

Writing Tests 65

Using Given-When-Then to Arrange a Test 66

Triangulation Method 69

Example: Function addition 69

How to Do Tasking with TDD 72

An Expression Parser for Tracking Progress 73

Applying TDD Step by Step 75

Keep Refactoring – Extract Functions to Files 78

Summary 80

Chapter 5: Project Setup 81

Application Requirements 81

Feature 1 – Book List 82

Feature 2 – Book Detail 83

Feature 3 – Searching 83

Feature 4 – Book Reviews 84

Create the Project 84

    Using create-react-app 84

    Material UI Library 88

    Install Cypress 91

    Commit Code to Version Control 95

Summary 96

Chapter 6: Implement the Book List 97

Acceptance Tests for Book List 97

    A List (of Books) 97

    Verify Book Name 99

    Refactoring – Extract Function 100

    Refactoring – Extract Component 103

Talk to the Backend Server 105

    Stub Server 106

    Async Request in Application 108

    Setup and Teardown 110

Adding a Loading Indicator 114

    Refactor First 114

    Define a React Hook 118

Unit Tests of the Bookish Application 120

    Unit Test with the React Testing Library 120

Summary 123

Chapter 7: Implementing the Book Detail View 125

Acceptance Tests 125

    Link to Detail Page 126

    Verify Book Title on Detail Page 126

    Frontend Routing 127

Unit Tests...132

    Refactoring..133

    Book Detail Page..137

    File Structure...139

Testing Data...141

User Interface Refinement...143

    Using Grid System...144

Handling Default Value...146

    A Failing Test with undefined 146

One Last Change?...149

Summary...150

Chapter 8: Searching by Keyword 153

Acceptance Test...153

    One Step Further 158

    What Have We Done? 162

Moving Forward – The Test Code Is As Important...............................163

Summary...167

Chapter 9: Introduction to State Management 169

State Management...170

    A Typical Scenario of Building UI 170

    Pub-Sub Pattern 171

    A Brief of Redux..172

    Decoupling Data and View...174

    The Formula: view = f(state) 176

Implementing State Management...178

    Environment Setup 178

    Define a Slice 179

Fetching Data from Remote...181

Define the Store...183

Migrate the Application 185

Book List Container 186

Refine the SearchBox 187

Test Individual Reducers 189

Book Details Slice 190

Do You Need a State Management Library?.......................................193

Summary...194

Chapter 10: Book Reviews...197

Business Requirements 198

Start with an Empty List..198

Rendering a Static List 200

Use the Review Component in BookDetail 201

Fulfill a Book Review Form 203

End-to-End Test..205

Define a Review Slice..207

Adjust the Stub Server for Book Reviews..209

Refactoring 214

Add More Fields 216

Review Editing 220

Save a Review – Action and Reducer 223

Integration All Together...227

Summary...230

Chapter 11: Behavior-Driven Development..**231**

   Play with Cucumber...232

      Install and Config cucumber Plugin..233

   Live Document with cucumber 235

      File Structure..235

      The First Feature Specification...235

      Define the Steps 236

      Book List..238

      Searching 240

      Review Page..242

   Summary..244

Appendix A: Background of Testing Strategies **245**

Appendix B: A Short Introduction to TypeScript **251**

Index..**259**

About the Author

Juntao Qiu is an accomplished software developer renowned for his expertise in producing high-quality and easily maintainable code. He is committed to helping individuals improve their code-writing abilities and generously shares his vast knowledge and experience through multiple platforms, including books such as this one and *Maintainable React* (Leanpub, 2022).

In addition, Juntao hosts a YouTube channel (`@icodeit.juntao`) where he provides valuable insights, tips, and best practices for writing clean code and performing refactoring. Juntao's goal is to empower developers, enabling them to reach their full potential and have a positive impact on the software development industry.

About the Technical Reviewers

Jeff Friesen is a freelance teacher and software developer with an emphasis on Java. In addition to authoring *Java I/O, NIO and NIO.2* (Apress) and *Java Threads and the Concurrency Utilities* (Apress), Jeff has written numerous articles on Java and other technologies (such as Android) for JavaWorld (JavaWorld.com) – now InfoWorld (`www.infoworld.com/category/java/`), informIT (InformIT.com), Java.net (no longer in existence), SitePoint (SitePoint.com), and other websites. Jeff can be contacted via his email address: `jefff@xplornet.ca`.

Alexander Nnakwue has a background in mechanical engineering and is a senior software engineer with over seven years of experience in various industries including payments, blockchain, and marketing technology. He is a published author for professional JavaScript, a technical writer, and a reviewer. He currently works as a software engineer at Konecranes with the digital experience team, working on machine data and industrial cranes.

In his spare time, he loves to listen to music and enjoys the game of soccer. He resides in Helsinki, Finland, with his lovely wife and son Kaobi.

Acknowledgments

I am profoundly grateful to my ThoughtWorks colleagues for their enthusiastic engagement and invaluable contributions during the development of this book. Our project discussions were a fountain of insight, enriching the narrative with an array of diverse perspectives. A special acknowledgment goes to Evan Bottcher for his meticulous review and for providing an eloquent foreword for the book.

Before embarking on the second edition, I reached out to my newsletter (`https://juntao.substack.com/`) subscribers with a survey, seeking their expectations for the new iteration. The response was overwhelming and deeply informative – my heartfelt thanks go out to those dedicated readers who took the time to provide their input.

I must extend my profound appreciation to the editorial team for their indispensable support throughout the second edition's journey. Their expert advice has proven invaluable in refining the text, and it's their tireless dedication that has brought this project to fruition.

Finally, upon first sharing my book's vision with my colleagues at ThoughtWorks, the outpouring of valuable feedback I received – spanning from minor typographical corrections to substantial technical suggestions – was truly overwhelming. In particular, on a cool morning in May 2020, I was greeted with an uplifting email from Hannah Bourke, who not only expressed her appreciation for the book but also offered her editing assistance as a native English speaker and fellow developer. Her subsequent pull requests offered not just high-quality language corrections but also insightful technical review comments from a learner's perspective.

ACKNOWLEDGMENTS

Furthermore, I am indebted to Martin Fowler, a distinguished developer and writer, who surprised me with detailed and insightful feedback on my initial draft. Although the content of the book has significantly evolved since that draft, the essence of his invaluable comments is still palpably present. Heeded his advice, I've trimmed nearly a quarter of the content to enhance clarity and readability, removed unrelated code snippets from examples, and provided more context around the code. Above all, the lesson of simplicity that I learned from Martin has been invaluable – emphasizing a thorough exploration of one topic at a time, rather than superficially touching upon every possible aspect.

In summary, the journey to this book's completion has been enriched by the collective wisdom and support of countless individuals. Their feedback, suggestions, and encouragement have been nothing short of invaluable, for which I am eternally grateful.

Foreword 1

Sometimes, I find it hard to believe that it's been more than two decades since Kent Beck published *Extreme Programming Explained* including Test-Driven Development (TDD) as a core practice. In the years since then, the use of automated testing has become quite commonplace, something that almost all developers are familiar with – however, the "Red-Green-Refactor" cycle of TDD is often missing. The reality is that building software test first is not easy or trivial in real-world software development and requires deliberate practice and usually someone experienced to learn from.

At ThoughtWorks, my role is Head of Engineering – responsible for the quality of the software that our teams produce for and with our clients. We set a high standard for the "internal" quality of the code we produce, wanting it to be maintainable and extensible so that it can quickly be changed with confidence. Test-Driven Development is a default practice in ThoughtWorks – our experience shows that the practice leads to better software design and good confidence from a comprehensive automated test suite.

In my years at ThoughtWorks, I've seen the phenomenal rise in the importance of JavaScript and browser applications. In 2010, we advised that the industry should treat JavaScript as a first-class language (`www.thoughtworks.com/radar/languages-and-frameworks/javascript-as-a-first-class-language`) on the ThoughtWorks Technology Radar, applying all of the same engineering rigor as other platforms. As one of the authors of the Technology Radar, I've seen and helped document the explosion of tooling and frameworks in JavaScript, many of which have been related to the area of test automation.

Test-Driven Development with React and TypeScript is a practical and hands-on guide to learn TDD with React, the most prevalent browser application framework in use today. It guides the reader through the fundamentals of TDD with React by implementing a series of requirements in a nontrivial example application. The book is fast-paced, so if you're unfamiliar with React and its friends, you'll need to pause along the way and do some research as the example application grows in features and dependencies. Along the way, Juntao points out some "smells" or signs that the approach can be improved – for example, cluttered code organization or hard-to-maintain test data.

Read this book if you would like to learn by example from someone who is an expert in using TDD to grow browser applications.

Evan Bottcher
March 2021

Foreword 2

Landing in the middle of a React project that had very low test coverage, in a team that had aspirations to improve it, but without a clear strategy of how to go about it, I struggled to find resources that stepped out how to approach testing for a frontend project. I couldn't find a clear explanation of how to implement Test-Driven Development for a UI, let alone specifically for React. This book couldn't have come at a better time.

There are a plethora of different testing methodologies and libraries available just for React. The ones you choose will depend on many things. This book doesn't prescribe a particular solution but establishes the purpose of tests in driving out specifications and suggests an overall approach, with practical guidance and examples. Juntao provides a holistic explanation of the purpose and implementation of Test-Driven Development for React, demonstrating the benefits of moving testing earlier in the process, improving the robustness and design of our code.

Juntao's years of experience, his eagerness and passion for learning and sharing his knowledge in a didactic way, help to make this a relevant, practical, and engaging guide to follow and have given me confidence in my own testing strategies.

Hannah Bourke
March 2021

Introduction

This comprehensive book is your ultimate guide to mastering Test-Driven Development (TDD) in the context of React and TypeScript. Whether you're a seasoned developer seeking to refine your skills or a newcomer eager to embrace industry-standard practices, this book caters to all levels of expertise.

Spanning a wide range of topics, each chapter in this book is thoughtfully designed to provide you with a deep understanding of TDD principles and their application in real-world scenarios. Let's take a glimpse into the chapters and their role in your learning journey:

Chapters 1 to 4: Setting Up the Foundation

In these early chapters, we lay the groundwork for your TDD journey. We provide a brief history of Test-Driven Development, allowing you to grasp the underlying concepts and motivations. You'll then dive into getting started with Jest, Cypress, and the React Testing Library, equipping you with the necessary tools to write effective tests.

Chapters 5 to 10: Implementing the Features

These chapters form the heart of the book, as we guide you through the step-by-step implementation of key features in our Bookish application. From building the book list and book detail view to incorporating search functionality, state management, and even enabling user reviews, you'll gain invaluable hands-on experience in applying TDD principles to build robust and reliable React applications.

Chapter 11: Describing Acceptance Tests

In this final chapter, we explore the concept of acceptance testing and introduce you to Behavior-Driven Development (BDD). You'll learn how to write acceptance tests that ensure your application meets the desired behavior and satisfies stakeholder requirements.

By following along with each chapter, you'll not only acquire the knowledge and skills to excel in TDD but also experience the benefits firsthand. Faster feedback cycles, improved code quality, enhanced collaboration, and the confidence to make changes and add new features are just a few of the advantages you'll gain.

Are you ready to embark on a transformative journey toward becoming a more confident, efficient, and skilled developer? *Test-Driven Development with React and TypeScript: Building Maintainable React Applications* is your comprehensive companion. Let the power of TDD guide your development process, elevate your coding skills, and lay the foundation for a successful career in software development. Get ready to dive in and unlock the full potential of TDD in your React projects.

CHAPTER 1

A Brief History of Test-Driven Development

My purpose in writing this chapter is not to copy and paste cliches from blogs or to make it seem like I was part of the historic events (such as the Agile Manifesto or Extreme Programming activities) that led to the creation of Test-Driven Development as a methodology – believe me, I'm not that old.

However, I do believe that providing context around the topics we'll be discussing in this book can be helpful. In this chapter, we'll explore the basic workflow of TDD and the various practical approaches used by different schools of thought. If you prefer to jump straight into the code, feel free to do so by navigating to the next chapter and getting your hands dirty.

What Is Test-Driven Development?

TDD is a software development methodology in which tests are written to drive the development of an application. It was developed/rediscovered by Kent Beck in the late 1990s as part of Extreme Programming[1] and was well discussed in his famous book *Test-Driven Development: By Example.*

---

[1] `https://martinfowler.com/bliki/ExtremeProgramming.html`

© Juntao Qiu 2023
J. Qiu, *Test-Driven Development with React and TypeScript*,
https://doi.org/10.1007/978-1-4842-9648-6_1

In his book, Kent Beck describes two essential rules:

- Write new code only if you first have a failing automated test

- Eliminate duplication

which leads to the steps of Red-Green-Refactor, which we will discuss soon. The ultimate goal for these two rules is to write (as Ron Jeffries describes) *clean code that works.*

The Red-Green-Refactor Cycle

Red-Green-Refactor is the core cycle of Test-Driven Development (TDD) methodology. The cycle involves the following steps:

1. *Red*: Write a failing test that describes the desired behavior of a specific feature or functionality. The test should not pass yet as the functionality has not yet been implemented.

2. *Green*: Write the minimum amount of production code necessary to make the failing test pass. The focus should be solely on passing the test, without worrying about code quality or design.

3. *Refactor*: Improve the design of the production code without changing its behavior, ensuring that all tests continue to pass. This step includes optimizing the code, removing duplication, and enhancing its overall quality.

The cycle repeats with each new feature or functionality, with the goal of producing high-quality code that meets the specified requirements and is maintainable over time. The Red-Green-Refactor cycle (Figure 1-1) emphasizes writing automated tests before writing any production code, ensuring that the code is continually tested and improved as it evolves.

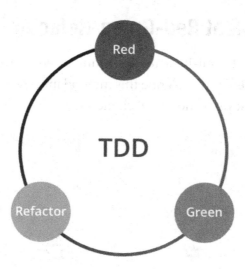

Figure 1-1. *Test-Driven Development*

At first glance, the principles may seem straightforward to follow. However, the challenge with many principles is that they may not work effectively for beginners. The principles are generally high level and challenging to implement, as they lack specificity and detailed guidance.

For example, just knowing the principles will not help you to answer questions like

- How can I write my very first test?

- What does enough code actually mean?

- When and how should I refactor?

- What refactoring techniques do I need to begin with?

This book aims to address these questions and equip you with the knowledge and skills necessary to apply these techniques with confidence in your daily workflow. By the end of the book, you should be well equipped to implement the discussed techniques effectively.

A Closer Look at Red-Green-Refactor

Examining the Red-Green-Refactor cycle more closely reveals something intriguing. To successfully integrate this method into our daily workflow, we must consider several additional elements.

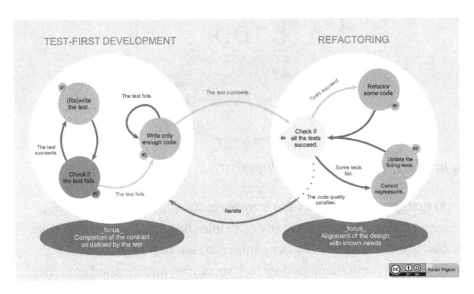

Figure 1-2. Test-Driven Development. Source: Wikipedia (https:// en.wikipedia.org/wiki/Test-driven_development)

Traditionally, TDD contains two major parts: quick implementation and then refactoring. In practice, the tests for quick implementation are not limited to the unit tests. They can be the acceptance tests as well – these are higher-level tests that focus more on business value and the end-user journey, without worrying too much about the technical details. Implementing the acceptance tests first could be an even better idea.

Starting with acceptance tests ensures that the right things are prioritized, and it provides confidence to developers when they want to clean up and refactor the code in the later stage. Acceptance tests are intended to be written from the end user's perspective; a passing acceptance test ensures the code meets the business requirement. Additionally, it protects the developer from wasting time on false assumptions or invalid requirements.

When applying TDD, you need to keep in mind a simple principle from Extreme Programming: YAGNI, or You Aren't Gonna Need It. YAGNI can be very useful for protecting developers from wasting their valuable time. Developers are very good at making assumptions around potential requirement changes, and based on those assumptions, they may come up with some unnecessary abstractions or optimizations that can make the code more generic or reusable. The problem is that those assumptions rarely turn out to be true. YAGNI emphasizes that you should not do it until you have to.

However, in the refactor phase, you can implement those abstractions and optimizations. Since you already have test coverage, it's much safer to do the cleanup then. Small refactors such as Change Class Name, Extract Method, or Extract Class to a higher level – anything that helps to make the code more generic and SOLID[2] are now safer and easier to undertake.

Types of TDD

Although TDD is a broad and diverse concept with many variations and different schools, such as UTDD, BDD, ATDD, and others, it traditionally implied Unit Test–Driven Development or UTDD. However, the TDD discussed in this book is an extended version of the conventional concept, known as Acceptance Test–Driven Development (ATDD), which places a strong emphasis on writing acceptance tests from the business perspective and using them to drive the development of production code.

---

[2] SOLID is an acronym for a set of principles in object-oriented design that promote maintainability, flexibility, and extensibility of software. Each letter in SOLID represents a principle: Single Responsibility Principle (SRP), Open/Closed Principle (OCP), Liskov Substitution Principle (LSP), Interface Segregation Principle (ISP) and Dependency Inversion Principle (DIP).

Having various tests in different layers can ensure that we are always on the right track and have the correct functionality.

Implementing Acceptance Test–Driven Development

To put it succinctly, ATDD defines the behavior of software from the end user's perspective by prioritizing the business value of the application rather than implementation details. Rather than validating that functions are called at specific times with correct parameters, ATDD ensures that when a user places an order, they receive their delivery on time.

We can merge the ATDD and UTDD into one diagram, as shown in Figure 1-3.

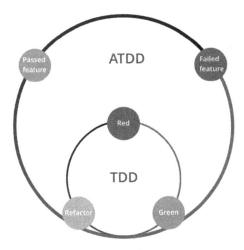

Figure 1-3. *Acceptance Test-Driven Development*

The diagram describes the following steps:

1. Write an acceptance test and see it fail.

2. Write a unit test and see it fail.

3. Write code to make the unit test pass.

4. Refactor the code.

5. Repeat steps 2–4, until acceptance test passes.

When you look at this process closely, you find that during the development stage, the acceptance test could be failing for quite some time. The feedback loop turns out to be very long, and there is a risk that an always-failed test means no test (protection) at all.

Developers could be confused about whether there are defects in the implementation or whether there is any implementation at all.

To resolve this problem, you have to write acceptance tests in relatively small chunks, testing a tiny slice of the requirement at a time. Alternatively, you could use the "fake it until you make it" approach, as we are going to use across this book.

The steps almost remain the same; only an extra fake step is added:

1. Write a failed acceptance test.

2. Make it pass in the most straightforward way (a fake implementation).

3. Refactor based on any code smells (like hard-coded data, magic number, etc.).

4. Add another new test based on a new requirement (if we need a new acceptance test, go back to step 1; otherwise, the process is just like traditional TDD).

Note that in the second step, you can use hard coding or a snippet of static HTML to make the test pass. At first glance, that may look redundant, but you will see the power of fake in the next few chapters.

The benefit of this variation is that when a developer is refactoring, there is always a passing acceptance test protecting you from breaking existing business logic. The drawback of this approach is that when a developer doesn't have enough experience, it can be difficult for them to come up with clean code designs – they could keep the fake in some way (e.g., a magic number, lack of abstractions, etc.).

Behavior-Driven Development

Another important variation of TDD is BDD, or Behavior-Driven Development. Behavior-Driven Development is an agile practice that encourages collaboration among different roles, developers, quality engineers, business analysts, or even other interested parties in a software project.

Although BDD is to some extent a general idea about how software development should be managed by both business interests and technical insight, the practice of BDD involves some specialized tools. For example, a Domain-Specific Language (DSL) is used to write tests in natural language that can be easily understood by nontechnical people and can be interpreted by code and executed behind the scenes.

The following code snippet of a BDD test case shows how a requirement can be described:

```
Given there are `10` books in the library
When a user visits the homepage
Then they would see `10` books on the page
And each book would contain at least `name`, `author`, `price`
and `rating`
```

We'll discuss this in detail in Chapter 10.

Prerequisites of TDD

To be candid, TDD can be a challenging methodology to apply. Several prerequisites must be met before implementing it effectively. A crucial prerequisite for TDD is a developer's ability to detect code smells and refactor them toward better design. Suppose, for example, you encounter smelly code, such as a lack of abstractions or magic numbers, and are unsure how to improve it. In that case, TDD alone may not be sufficient. While the TDD workflow must be followed, there is a risk of creating unmaintainable tests in addition to producing low-quality code.

Be Aware of Code Smell and Refactoring

In his book *Refactoring: Improving the Design of Existing Code*, Martin Fowler listed 68 refactorings. I would recommend this book as almost a mandatory prerequisite for anyone who values clean code and high-quality code. But don't worry too much, some of the refactorings he mentioned you may have already used in your daily work.

As mentioned earlier, a typical TDD workflow has three steps:

- A test case description requirement (specification)

- Some code to make the test pass

- Refactor the implementation and tests

It is a common misconception that test code is secondary or does not hold the same level of importance as production code. However, I would contend that test code is equally as crucial as production code. Maintainable tests are crucial to people who have to make changes later on or add new ones. Every time you refactor, make sure the changes made in the production code are reflected in the test code.

Test First or Test Last

The hardest part of applying TDD in your daily workflow is that you have to write tests before you start writing any production code. For most developers, that's not just different and counterintuitive but also breaks their own way of working significantly.

Nevertheless, the key to applying TDD is that you should build the fast feedback mechanism first. Once you have it, it doesn't matter much if you write the test first or last. By fast feedback, I mean that a method or an if-else branch can be tested in a very lightweight and effortless manner. If you add tests after all the functionality has been completed, you are not doing TDD by any means. Because you are missing the essential fast feedback loop – seen as the most important thing in development – you may also be missing the benefits promised by TDD.

9

By implementing a fast feedback loop, TDD ensures you are always on the right track – safely. It also gives you sufficient confidence to do the further code cleanup. And proper code cleanup can lead to a better code design. Of course, the cleanup does not come automatically, it requires extra time and effort. However, TDD is a great mechanism to protect you from breaking the application when you are making changes.

Other Techniques That Can Help Implement TDD

For the beginner, it can be challenging when applying TDD as it sometimes feels counterintuitive to test first. In practice, there are common reasons for resistance to TDD:

- For simple tasks, they don't need TDD.

- For complicated tasks, setting up the TDD mechanism itself can be too difficult.

There are a lot of tutorials and articles out there to describe techniques you should use to do TDD, and some may even involve describing how to split tasks before implementing TDD. However, things discussed in those tutorials are often oversimplified and can be hard to apply to a real-world project directly.

For example, in a web application, both the interaction and a considerable portion of business logic now exist in the frontend: the UI. The traditional techniques of how to write a unit test to drive backend logic are already outdated.

Tasking

Another critical skill required by TDD is splitting a large requirement into smaller chunks through tasking. I would suggest every developer should learn how to split requirements before they even start to write their first test.

We'll discuss the tasking process in detail in the next chapter.

Maintaining a Simple Checklist

Usually, we can stop at the second round of splitting, since the Red-Green-Refactor is far too detailed in terms of tasking. And too granular tasks means more management effort (tracking those tasks needs more energy). To make the tasks visible, we can put it down on a post-it note and mark a simple tick once it's done (Figure 1-4).

By using this simple tool, you can then focus on what you're going to do and make the progress more accurate when you want to update it to other team members (e.g., in the daily stand-up meeting). By saying a task is 50% done, half of the items on the list are ticked off on the list you made earlier.

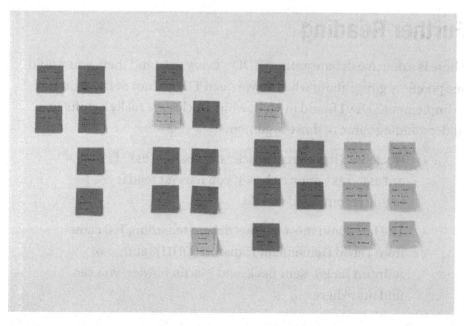

Figure 1-4. *Tasking with sticky notes*

Summary

Refactoring depends on the sense and experience of identifying code smells. Once you find a code smell, you can then apply the corresponding refactoring technique. And then we may achieve maintainable, human-readable, extendable, and clean code along the way.

In the next chapter, we will introduce a concrete example to demonstrate how to apply TDD step by step. Along with that example, we will also cover the fundamental skills needed for implementing TDD, including how to use the jest testing framework and how to do tasking with real-world examples.

Further Reading

There is extensive debate around TDD – every now and then, you would see people arguing about whether we need TDD or not or the right way to implement TDD. I found the following articles are really helpful in understanding some of those arguments:

- Uncle Bob has a great article[3] discussing test first or test last approaches. If you haven't read it yet, I highly recommend you do.

- The latest and most famous debate regarding TDD came from David Heinemeier Hansson (DHH) (author of Ruby on Rails), Kent Beck, and Martin Fowler; you can find more here.[4]

---

[3] https://blog.cleancoder.com/uncle-bob/2016/11/10/TDD-Doesnt-work.html
[4] https://martinfowler.com/articles/is-tdd-dead/

Also, I highly recommend reading these books to build a solid foundation for implementing TDD. Even if you decided not to utilize TDD, these books are still highly recommended:

- *Clean Code: A Handbook of Agile Software Craftsmanship* by Robert C. Martin[5]

- *Refactoring: Improving the Design of Existing Code* by Martin Fowler[6]

---

[5] www.goodreads.com/book/show/3735293-clean-code
[6] https://martinfowler.com/books/refactoring.html

CHAPTER 2

Get Started with Jest

In this chapter, we'll explore the key concepts and features of Jest,[1] a popular JavaScript testing framework. We'll cover different types of `matchers`, as well as the powerful and flexible `expect` and the useful mock for unit testing. Moreover, we'll learn how to organize our test suite in a manner that's easy to maintain, and we'll explore best practices drawn from real-world projects. By the end of the chapter, you'll have a solid understanding of Jest's capabilities and how to use it effectively in your own projects.

We will be using ES6 as the primary programming language throughout this book.

To start off, we'll walk you through setting up your environment to write your first test. Throughout this book, we'll be using ES6 as the primary programming language.

Set Up the Environment

To follow along with the examples in this book, you'll need to install `node.js`, which we'll be using as the primary platform. If you're using a `MacOS` with `homebrew`, you can install `node` by running the following command:

```
brew install node
```

---

[1] `https://jestjs.io/`

© Juntao Qiu 2023
J. Qiu, *Test-Driven Development with React and TypeScript*,
https://doi.org/10.1007/978-1-4842-9648-6_2

If you're running a different operating system or prefer another option, you can download node from here.[2]

Once you have node installed locally, you can use npm (Node Package Manager) to install node packages. npm is a binary program that comes bundled with the node runtime.

Install and Configure Jest

Jest is a testing framework from Facebook that allows developers to write reliable and fast-running tests in a more readable syntax. It can watch changes in test/source files and rerun the necessary tests automatically. This allows you to get quick feedback, and that is a crucial factor in TDD. The speed of feedback can even determine whether TDD works for you or not. Simply put, the faster tests can run, the more efficient developers can be.

Let's firstly create a folder for our experiment and initialize the folder with a package.json to maintain all the following package installations:

```
mkdir jest-101
cd jest-101
npm init -y #init the current folder with default settings
```

When you install jest as a development dependency, it means that jest is only needed during the development phase of your project and is not required in the final production package. This helps to keep your production package lean and focused on the essential components that your users need.

```
npm install --save-dev jest
```

---

[2] https://nodejs.org/en/download

After the installation, you can run jest --init to specify some default settings, such as where jest should find the test files and the source code, which environment (there are a lot) jest should run against (browser or node for the backend), and so on. You have to answer some questions to let jest understand your requirements; for now, let's just accept all the default settings by saying Yes for all the questions.

Note that if you have installed jest globally (with npm install jest -g), you can use the following command to init the config directly:

```
jest --init
```

Otherwise, you will have to use the local installation by npx, which looks for jest binary from node_modules/.bin/ and invokes it:

```
npx jest --init
```

For the sake of simplicity, we use node as a test environment, without coverage report, and all other default settings like so:

```
npx jest --init
```

The following questions will help Jest to create a suitable configuration for your project:

```
✔ Would you like to use Typescript for the configuration
file? ... no
✔ Choose the test environment that will be used for
testing › node
✔ Do you want Jest to add coverage reports? ... no
✔ Which provider should be used to instrument code for
coverage? › v8
✔ Automatically clear mock calls, instances, contexts and
results before every test? ... no
📝 Configuration file created at /Users/juntao/icodeit/ideas/
jest-101/jest.config.js
```

To use TypeScript with `jest-101`, we need to first install and configure babel. If you're not familiar with `babel`, don't worry – we'll cover it in the next chapter. In essence, `babel` is a tool that can translate TypeScript to JavaScript that can be understood by the JavaScript runtime (Node).

```
npm install --save-dev babel-jest @babel/core @babel/preset-env
```

And then create a `babel.config.js` file in the root of our project (the jest-101 folder), with the following content:

```
module.exports = {
  presets: [['@babel/preset-env', {targets: {node: 'current'}}]],
};
```

Now let's enable TypeScript for our source code:

```
npm install --save-dev @babel/preset-typescript
```

And modify `babel.config.js` with the following content:

```
module.exports = {
  presets: [
    ['@babel/preset-env', {targets: {node: 'current'}}],
    '@babel/preset-typescript',
  ],
};
```

We're all set now. It's time to write our first Jest test.

Jest at First Glance

Cool, we're ready to write some tests to verify that all parts can work together now. Let's create a folder named `src` and put two files in `calc.test.ts` and `calc.ts`.

The file ends with "test.ts", that means it's a pattern that jest will recognize and treat them as tests, as defined in the jest.config.js we generated previously:

```
// The glob patterns Jest uses to detect test files
// testMatch: [
//   "**/__tests__/**/*.[jt]s?(x)",
//   "**/?(*.)+(spec|test).[tj]s?(x)"
// ],
```

Note the previous configuration is the default generated one, and you can modify it to support other file name patterns. We'll keep it as is because ts is already included.

Let's add some code to our calc.test.ts file:

```
import { add } from "./calc";

describe("calculator", function () {
  it("should be able to add two numbers", function () {
    expect(add(1, 2)).toEqual(3);
  });
});
```

In Jest, the describe function is used to group related tests together and create a logical structure within your test suite. It provides a way to organize and categorize tests based on a specific functionality, component, or feature. And the it function, also known as a test case or a spec, is used to define an individual test within your test suite. It represents a specific scenario or behavior that you want to verify in your code.

The describe function takes two arguments: a description string and a callback function. The description string is typically a brief explanation of what the tests in that group are targeting. The callback function contains the actual tests or nested describe blocks.

The it function takes two arguments: a description string and a callback function. The description string describes what behavior or outcome you are testing. The callback function contains the actual test assertions or expectations.

In our example, the assertion expect(add(1, 2)).toEqual(3) checks whether the result of calling the add function with arguments 1 and 2 is equal to 3.

The function add is imported from another file and is implemented like this:

```
function add(x: number, y: number) {
  return x + y;
}

export { add };
```

To run the test and check the result:

```
npm run test
```

And you would see something like this:

```
npm run test

> jest-101@1.0.0 test
> jest

 PASS  src/calc.test.ts
  calculator
    ✓ add two numbers (1 ms)

Test Suites: 1 passed, 1 total
Tests:       1 passed, 1 total
Snapshots:   0 total
Time:        0.259 s, estimated 1 s
Ran all test suites.
```

Fantastic, we now have our very first test up and running!

Basic Concepts in Jest

By utilizing the power of describe and it, you can structure your test suite, enhance readability, and convey the intent of your tests more effectively. These functions form the building blocks for creating comprehensive and well-organized test suites in Jest. Let's dive into the world of Jest testing and harness the full potential of describe and it to ensure the quality and reliability of your code.

Jest API: describe and it

For example, we can put all arithmetic into one group:

```
describe("calculator", () => {
  it("should perform addition", () => {});
  it("should perform subtraction", () => {});
  it("should perform multiplication", () => {});
  it("should perform division", () => {});
});
```

What's more, we can nest describe functions like so:

```
describe("calculator", () => {
  describe("should perform addition", () => {
    it("adds two positive numbers", () => {});
    it("adds two negative numbers", () => {});
    it("adds one positive and one negative numbers", () => {});
  });
});
```

The fundamental idea is to group relevant tests together, so that the test descriptions make sense for those who maintain them. It's even more helpful if you can describe the description (the first parameter for the describe and it functions) using domain language within a business context. This way, the test suite is easier to understand and more closely aligned with the needs of the stakeholders who will ultimately benefit from the software being tested.

Organize Your Tests Maintainer Friendly

For instance, when you are developing a hotel reservation application, the tests read like this:

```
describe("Hotel Sunshine", () => {
  describe("Reservation", () => {
    it("should make a reservation when there are enough rooms
    available", () => {});
    it("should warn the administrator when there are only 5
    available rooms left", () => {});
  });

  describe("Checkout", () => {
    it("should check if any appliance is broken", () => {});
    it("should refund guest when checkout is earlier than
    planned", () => {});
  });
});
```

You may occasionally find some duplicated code scattered in test cases, for example, setting up a subject in each test is not uncommon:

```
describe("addition", () => {
  it("adds two positive numbers", () => {
    const options = {
      precision: 2,
    };
```

```
  const calc = new Calculator(options);
  const result = calc.add(1.333, 3.2);
  expect(result).toEqual(4.53);
});

it("adds two negative numbers", () => {
  const options = {
    precision: 2,
  };

  const calc = new Calculator(options);
  const result = calc.add(-1.333, -3.2);
  expect(result).toEqual(-4.53);
  });
});
```

Set Up and Tear Down

To reduce duplication, we can utilize the beforeEach function provided
by Jest to define reusable object instances. This function is automatically
invoked before Jest runs each test case. In our case, the calculator
instance can be used in all the test cases within the same describe block,
making it a convenient and efficient way to reduce repetition in our code:

```
describe("addition", () => {
  let calc = null;

  beforeEach(() => {
    const options = {
      precision: 2,
    };
    calc = new Calculator(options);
  });
```

```
it("adds two positive numbers", () => {
  const result = calc.add(1.333, 3.2);
  expect(result).toEqual(4.53);
});

it("adds two negative numbers", () => {
  const result = calc.add(-1.333, -3.2);
  expect(result).toEqual(-4.53);
});
});
```

You might be wondering if there is a corresponding function named afterEach or if there is a way to handle cleanup tasks. The answer is yes! Jest provides an afterEach function that can be used to perform any necessary cleanup work after each test case has been run:

```
describe("database", () => {
  let db = null;

  beforeEach(() => {
    db.connect("localhost", "9999", "user", "pass");
  });

  afterEach(() => {
    db.disconnect();
  });
});
```

In this example, we are setting up a database connection before each test case and closing it down afterward. In a real-world scenario, you might also want to add a function to roll back any database changes or perform other cleanup tasks in the afterEach step.

Furthermore, if you need something to be set up before all the test cases start and then torn down after all of them are finished, you can use the beforeAll and afterAll functions provided by Jest:

```
beforeAll(() => {
  db.connect("localhost", "9999", "user", "pass");
});

afterAll(() => {
  db.disconnect();
});
```

Using Matchers in Jest

Jest offers a variety of helper functions (matchers) that developers can use for assertions when writing tests. These matchers allow you to test various data types in different scenarios. We'll start with some basic examples and then move on to more advanced ones later on.

Basic Usages

Equality

toEqual and toBe may be the most common matchers you will find and use in almost every test case. As the name implies, they are used to assert whether values are equal to each other (the actual value and the expected value).

For example, it can be used for string, number, or composed objects:

```
it("basic usage", () => {
  expect(1 + 1).toEqual(2);
  expect("Juntao").toEqual("Juntao");
  expect({ name: "Juntao" }).toEqual({ name: "Juntao" });
});
```

25

and for toBe:

```
it("basic usage", () => {
  expect(1 + 1).toBe(2); // PASS
  expect("Juntao").toBe("Juntao"); // PASS
  expect({ name: "Juntao" }).toBe({ name: "Juntao" }); //FAIL
});
```

The last test will fail. For primitives like strings, numbers, and booleans, you can use toBe to test the equality. While for Objects, internally jest uses Object.is to check, which is strict and compares objects by memory address. So if you want to make sure all the fields are matching, use toEqual.

.not Method for Opposite Matching

Jest also provides .not that you can use to assert the opposite value:

```
it("basic usage", () => {
  expect(1 + 2).not.toEqual(2);
});
```

Sometimes, you might not want an exact match. Say you want a string to be matching some particular pattern. Then you can use toMatch instead:

```
it("match regular expression", () => {
  expect("juntao").toMatch(/\w+/);
});
```

In fact, you can write any valid regular expression:

```
it("match numbers", () => {
  expect("185-3345-3343").toMatch(/^\d{3}-\d{4}-\d{4}$/);
  expect("1853-3345-3343").not.toMatch(/^\d{3}-\d{4}-\d{4}$/);
});
```

Jest makes it very easy to work with strings. However, you can use comparisons with numbers too:

```
it("compare numbers", () => {
  expect(1 + 2).toBeGreaterThan(2);
  expect(1 + 2).toBeGreaterThanOrEqual(2);

  expect(1 + 2).toBeLessThan(4);
  expect(1 + 2).toBeLessThanOrEqual(4);
});
```

Matchers for Array and Object

Jest also provides matchers for Array and Object.

toContainEqual and toContain

For instance, it's quite common to test if an element is contained in an Array:

```
const users = ["Juntao", "Abruzzi", "Alex"];

it("match arrays", () => {
  expect(users).toContainEqual("Juntao");
  expect(users).toContain(users[0]);
});
```

Note that there is a difference between toContain and toContainEqual. Basically, toContain checks if the item is in the list by strictly comparing elements using ===. On the other hand, toContainEqual just checks the value (not the memory address).

For example, if you want to check whether an object is in a list:

```
it("object in array", () => {
  const users = [{ name: "Juntao" }, { name: "Alex" }];
  expect(users).toContainEqual({ name: "Juntao" }); // PASS
  expect(users).toContain({ name: "Juntao" }); // FAIL
});
```

The second assertion would fail since it uses a more strict comparison. As an object is just a combination of other JavaScript primitives, we can use dot notion and test the existence of the field or use the preceding matchers for fields in an object:

```
it("match object", () => {
  const user = {
    name: "Juntao",
    address: "Xian, Shaanxi, China",
  };

  expect(user.name).toBeDefined();
  expect(user.age).not.toBeDefined();
});
```

The Powerful Function expect

We have briefly seen the power of matcher in the previous sections. Now, let's explore another powerful tool provided by Jest: the expect object.

The expect object comes with several useful helper functions, such as

- expect.stringContaining

- expect.arrayContaining

- expect.objectContaining

Using these functions, you can create your own custom `matchers`. For example:

```
it("string contains", () => {
  const givenName = expect.stringContaining("Juntao");
  expect("Juntao Qiu").toEqual(givenName);
});
```

The variable `givenName` here is not a simple value, it's a new matcher and matches strings containing `Juntao`.

Similarly, you can use `arrayContaining` to check a subset of an array:

```
describe("array", () => {
  const users = ["Juntao", "Abruzzi", "Alex"];

  it("array containing", () => {
    const userSet = expect.arrayContaining(["Juntao", "Abruzzi"]);
    expect(users).toEqual(userSet);
  });
});
```

It looks a bit strange at first glance, but once you understand it, that pattern would help you to build more complicated matchers.

For instance, say we retrieve some data from the backend API, with a payload that looks like

```
interface User {
  name: string;
  address: string;
  projects: Project[];
}

interface Project {
  name: string;
}
```

```
const user: User = {
  name: "Juntao Qiu",
  address: "Xian, Shaanxi, China",
  projects: [
    { name: "ThoughtWorks University" },
    { name: "ThoughtWorks Core Business Beach" },
  ],
};
```

For whatever reason, in our test we don't care about address at all. We do care if the name field contains Juntao and the project.name contains ThoughtWorks.

The containing Family Functions

So let's define a matcher by using the stringContaining, arrayContaining, and objectContaining like so:

```
const matcher = expect.objectContaining({
  name: expect.stringContaining("Juntao"),
  projects: expect.arrayContaining([
    { name: expect.stringContaining("ThoughtWorks") },
  ]),
});
```

This expression describes exactly what we expect, and we can then use toEqual to do the assertion:

```
expect(user).toEqual(matcher)
```

As you can see, this pattern is pretty powerful. Basically, you can define a matcher just as you would in natural language. It could even be used in a contract between frontend and backend services.

Build Your Matchers

Jest also allows you to extend the expect object to define your own matchers. In that way, you can enhance the default matcher set and make the test code more readable.

Let's see a concrete example in this section. We'll use a package called jsonpath to extract data from JSON objects or to transform JSON data using JSONPath expressions.

JSONPath is a query language used for searching and manipulating JSON data. It's similar to XPath, which is used for searching XML data, but JSONPath is specifically designed for JSON data.

Example: jsonpath Matcher

Firstly, let's install jsonpath to the project root jest-101:

```
npm install jsonpath --save
```

And then use it like this:

```
import jsonpath from "jsonpath";

const user = {
  name: "Juntao Qiu",
  address: "Xian, Shaanxi, China",
  projects: [
    { name: "ThoughtWorks University" },
    { name: "ThoughtWorks Core Business Beach" },
  ],
};

const result = jsonpath.query(user, "$.projects");
console.log(JSON.stringify(result));
```

And you will get the result:

```
[
  [
    { name: "ThoughtWorks University" },
    { name: "ThoughtWorks Core Business Beach" },
  ],
]
```

and query `$.projects[0].name`

```
const result = jsonpath.query(user, '$.projects[0].name')
```

would get

```
["ThoughtWorks University"]
```

The query would return an empty array ([ ]) if the path didn't match anything:

```
const result = jsonpath.query(user, '$.projects[0].address')
```

Extend the expect Function

Let's define a matcher named toMatchJsonPath as an extension by using function expect.extend:

```
import jsonpath from "jsonpath";

expect.extend({
  toMatchJsonPath(received, argument) {
    const result = jsonpath.query(received, argument);

    if (result.length > 0) {
      return {
        pass: true,
```

```
      message: () => "matched",
    };
  } else {
    return {
      pass: false,
      message: () =>
        `expected ${JSON.stringify(received)} to match
        jsonpath ${argument}`,
    };
  }
  },
});
```

So internally, Jest would pass two parameters to the customizing matcher. The first one is the actual result – the one you pass to function expect(). The second one, on the other hand, is the expected value you passed to the matcher, which in our case is toMatchJsonPath.

For the return value, it's a simple JavaScript object that contains pass, which is a boolean value that indicates whether the test passes or not, and a message field to describe the reason for the pass or fail, respectively.

Once defined, you can use it in your test just like any other built-in matchers:

```
describe("jsonpath", () => {
  it("matches jsonpath", () => {
    const user = {
      name: "Juntao",
    };
    expect(user).toMatchJsonPath("$.name");
  });
```

```
  it("does not match jsonpath", () => {
    const user = {
      name: "Juntao",
      address: "ThoughtWorks",
    };
    expect(user).not.toMatchJsonPath("$.age");
  });
});
```

Impressive, isn't it? This technique can be very handy in making your matcher more readable, especially when you want to use a Domain-Specific Language.

For example:

```
const employee = {};
expect(employee).toHaveName("Juntao");
expect(employee).toBelongToDepartment("Product Halo");
```

Mocking and Stubbing

During unit testing, it is often preferable to avoid making actual calls to underlying external functions. In such cases, we can make use of a technique called mocking where we simply simulate the function call rather than actually invoking it. For instance, when testing email template functionality, we may not want to send an email to a real client. Instead, we can test whether the HTML generated contains the correct content or verify that an email was sent to a specific address. Similarly, connecting to a production database to test the deletion API would not be acceptable in most scenarios.

And in Jest, there are many ways to do the mocking.

jest.fn for Spying

So we, as developers, need to set up a mechanism to enable this. Jest provides a variety of ways to do this mock. The simplest one is function jest.fn for setting up a spy for a function:

```
it("create a callable function", () => {
  const mock = jest.fn();
  mock("Juntao");
  expect(mock).toHaveBeenCalled();
  expect(mock).toHaveBeenCalledWith("Juntao");
  expect(mock).toHaveBeenCalledTimes(1);
});
```

You can use jest.fn() to create a function that could be invoked just like other regular functions, except it provides the ability to be audited. A mock can track all the invocations to it. And it can record the invoke times, and the parameter passed in for each invoke. That could be very useful, since in many scenarios we just want to ensure the particular function has been called with specified parameters and in the correct order – we don't have to do the real invoke.

Mock Implementation

A dummy mock object as seen in the previous example doesn't do anything interesting. The following one is more meaningful:

```
it("mock implementation", () => {
  const fakeAdd = jest.fn().mockImplementation((a, b) => 5);

  expect(fakeAdd(1, 1)).toBe(5);
  expect(fakeAdd).toHaveBeenCalledWith(1, 1);
});
```

Instead of defining a static mock, you can define an implementation by yourself too. The real implementation could be very complicated; maybe it does some calculation based on a complex formula on some given parameters.

Stub a Remote Service Call

Additionally, just imagine we have a function that invokes a remote API call to fetch data:

```
export const fetchUser = (id: string, process: () => void) => {
  return fetch(`http://localhost:4000/users/${id}`);
};
```

In the test code, especially in a unit test, we don't want to perform any remote calls, so we use mock instead. In this example, we're testing that our function fetchUser will call the global fetch:

```
describe("mock API call", () => {
  const user = {
    name: "Juntao",
  };

  it("mock fetch", () => {
    // given
    global.fetch = jest
      .fn()
      .mockImplementation(() => Promise.resolve({ user }));
    const process = jest.fn();

    // when
    fetchUser(111).then((x) => console.log(x));
```

```
  // then
  expect(global.fetch).toHaveBeenCalledWith(
    "http://localhost:4000/users/111"
  );
});
});
```

We expect that the `fetch` is invoked by `http://localhost:4000/users/111`; note the `id` we are using here. And we can see that the user information is printed out on the console:

```
PASS  src/advanced/matcher.test.ts
  ● Console

  console.log src/advanced/matcher.test.js:152
    { user: { name: 'Juntao' } }
```

That is something very useful. `Jest` provides other mock mechanisms as well, but we are not going to discuss them here. We are not using any advanced features in this book other than what we have addressed earlier.

If you are interested, please check `jest` help or home page for more information.

Summary

In this chapter, we've covered the fundamentals of `jest`, including its essential features like test blocks, matchers, and the `expect` object. Building upon this foundation, the upcoming chapter will delve deeper into Test-Driven Development (TDD) with `jest`. TDD is a highly effective technique that enables us to write higher-quality code and detect bugs at an early stage. With `jest`, we'll discover the process of writing tests before code and utilizing them as a guide throughout development. Prepare yourself for an exciting journey of advancing your development skills to new heights!

CHAPTER 3

Refactoring Essentials: The Basics You Need to Know

Before we dive into Test-Driven Development, let's discuss some common refactorings that we will be utilizing throughout this book. These refactorings may seem small on the surface and may not appear to do much, but mastering them can make you a more effective programmer. It's not just about how fast you can type but also how quickly you can mold and reshape your code to prevent losing the ideas you have in your mind.

I have compiled a list of the most common refactorings I use daily, and they will be presented in this section.

The Ten Most Common Refactorings

Like in many other fields, the 20/80 rule applies in refactoring as well. In case you're wondering, Martin Fowler, in his book *Refactoring: Improving the Design of Existing Code*, described around 48 common refactorings, and 20% of them is (20% * 48 = 9.6) roughly 10, which we'll cover in this chapter.

© Juntao Qiu 2023
J. Qiu, *Test-Driven Development with React and TypeScript*,
https://doi.org/10.1007/978-1-4842-9648-6_3

Let's Talk the Problem – Code Smells

Any fool can write code that a computer can understand. Good programmers write code that humans can understand.

—Martin Fowler

The following are some common code smells or symptoms that I've encountered in various projects:

- Meaningless names

- Long files

- Excessively large props list (React)

- Mixing computation with views (React)

- Overuse of mocks

- Not adhering to established principles

Eliminating these symptoms can greatly improve the readability and maintainability of our code, which is crucial for clean code. In the following sections, we will discuss each of these symptoms in detail.

Long Files

The long file code smell refers to a situation where a single file in a codebase becomes excessively long, often containing multiple functions, classes, and other components. Long files can be difficult to navigate, understand, and maintain and can lead to issues such as code duplication, decreased performance, and reduced readability. It is generally considered a best practice to keep files as small and focused as possible and to split them into separate files if they become too large.

Big Props List

The Big Props List issue refers to a problem that arises when a React component receives a large number of props. This can make the component's code difficult to read, understand, and maintain over time. It's bad because it violates the Single Responsibility Principle and can lead to tightly coupled components that are hard to reuse or refactor. Additionally, passing too many props can cause performance issues, as React needs to re-render the component every time any of its props change.

```
const BasketContainer = ({
  testID,
  orderData,
  basketError,
  addCoupon,
  voucherSelected,
  validationErrors,
  clearErrors,
  removeLine,
  editLine,
  hideOrderButton,
  hideEditButton,
  loading,
}: BasketContainerProps)
```

It's normal that programmers tend to put related code together, and that's seemingly the effortless one. But in my experience, that's the most expensive mistake you can ever make.

There are many reasons why a large file is bad. Firstly, it's hard to read and understand. Let's admire that most of our development work is about understanding the existing code rather than composing new code.

Secondly, the impact of your change is not predictable when it's large. The longer a file, the harder it becomes to understand. And a large file also means it tries to do too many things in one place, or you can call it lack of abstraction.

Mixing Computation with Views

Mixing computation with rendering logic in React can make the code less modular, harder to test, and less reusable. It can also make it more difficult to understand the code and to make changes without introducing new bugs. Additionally, it can lead to performance issues as the rendering process may take longer due to the extra computations when re-rendering (which can be more frequent than you think).

```
const Order = () => {
  const { t } = useTranslation('order');

  const serviceText = serviceMethod === 'Pickup' ? t('PickUp')
  : t('Deliver');

  const storeNameOrDeliveryAddress =
    serviceMethod === 'Pickup'
      ? selectedStore && selectedStore.media.name
      : selectedDeliveryAddress === undefined || '' ||
      !selectedDeliveryAddress.displayAddress
        ? t('DeliveryAddressNotAvailable')
        : selectedDeliveryAddress.displayAddress;

  return <div>
    {...}
  </div>
}
```

Overuse of Mocks

Sometimes, you may see a long list of mocks in each test file or maybe a
long beforeEach or afterEach. Or in other cases, you may see the tests are
verifying data structures rather than behaviors, but they all fit the hard to
test category.

```
const mockUseLocation = jest.fn().mockImplementation(() => ({
state: {} }))

jest.mock('@reach/router', () => ({
  ...jest.requireActual<{}>('@reach/router'),
  navigate: jest.fn(),
  useLocation: mockUseLocation,
}))

const mockShowAlert = jest.fn()
jest.mock('@company/hooks-and-hocs', () => ({
  ...jest.requireActual<{}>('@company/hooks-and-hocs'),

  useSdkAvailable: jest.fn().mockImplementation(() => ({
    found: true,
  })),

  useAlert: jest.fn().mockImplementation(() => ({
    showAlert: mockShowAlert,
  })),

  //...
}))
```

Using too many mocks in testing can be a bad idea for several reasons:

- *It can lead to false positives*: Mocks are used to simulate certain functionality, but they are not the real thing. This means that if there is a problem with the real functionality that is not reflected in the mock, your tests may give you a false sense of security.

- *It can lead to brittle tests*: If the code under test changes in a way that requires changes to the mocks, you may have to update a lot of tests, which can be time-consuming and error-prone.

- *It can make tests harder to read and maintain*: If you have too many mocks, your tests can become difficult to understand and maintain, which can lead to errors and wasted time.

Not Following Established Principles

In the not-so-long history of the computer science and software engineering industry, we have many proven design principles, for instance, SOLID, Don't Repeat Yourself, You Aren't Gonna Need It, and so on. Often, the unclean code can be avoided by simply following these principles or patterns.

Unfortunately, many developers do not pay too much attention to these principles and, for whatever reason, just put the code together and try to make the application run. To be honest, many software I've seen in projects are not designed but only put together and hoped it would work.

All right, let's get started with an existing implementation of ROT13 first.

The Problem – ROT13

So the code snippet we're using in this chapter implements ROT13. ROT13, or "rotate by 13 places," is a simple letter substitution cipher that replaces a letter with the 13th letter after it in the alphabet. So A becomes N, B to O, and so on till M to Z. And then it looks backward, so N becomes A and O becomes B and so on.

In this chapter, we'll focus on one implementation of ROT13 and try to apply different refactorings (with WebStorm shortcuts for demonstration) to make it a better version.

The Initial Implementation

So we have already got an implementation here; it definitely has room for improvement, but it works and can make all the tests pass:

```
export const convert = (str: string) => {
  const letters = "ABCDEFGHIJKLMNOPQRSTUVWXYZ";

  return str.split("")
    .map((c) => {
      const index = letters.indexOf(c);
      if (index !== -1) {
        if (index + 13 >= 26) {
          return letters[index + 13 - 26];
        } else {
          return letters[index + 13];
        }
      }
      return c;
    }).join("");
};
```

where the corresponding tests are

- Returns N when given A

- Returns A when given N

- Returns NO when given AB (multiple letters)

- Returns AB!! when given NO!! (keep other symbols as is while converting)

Before we make any code changes, let's run these tests first:

```
describe("ROT13", () => {
  it("returns N when given A", () => {
    expect(convert("A")).toEqual("N");
  });

  it("return A when given N", () => {
    expect(convert("N")).toEqual("A");
  });

  it("return NO when given AB", () => {
    expect(convert("AB")).toEqual("NO");
  });

  it("return AB!! when given NO!!", () => {
    expect(convert("NO!!")).toEqual("AB!!");
  });
});
```

And now all the tests are passing fine.

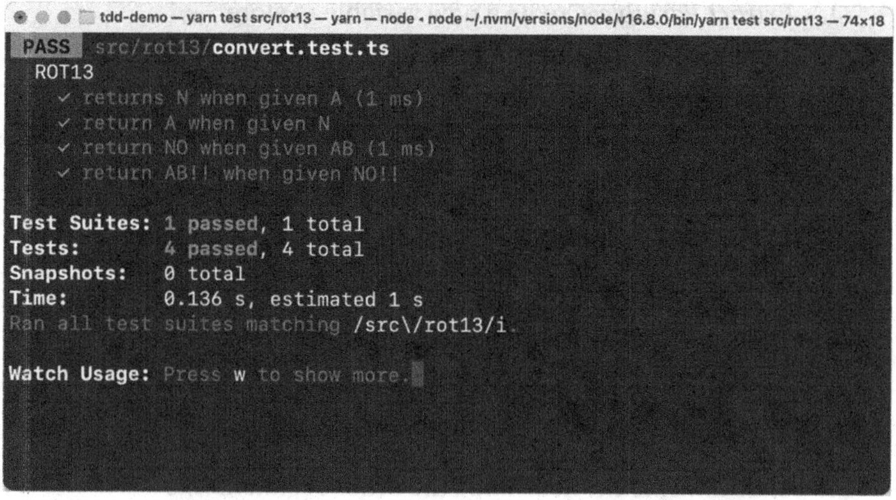

Figure 3-1. *Unit tests are all passing*

In the upcoming sections, we will examine the preceding implementation and employ commonly used refactorings using WebStorm shortcuts to transform the code into a maintainable condition. You may use any text editor or IDE of your preference to accomplish the task.

The Top Ten Refactorings

The refactorings we'll discuss in this chapter will be

1. *Rename Variable*: Change the name of a variable to improve clarity and readability.

2. *Change Function Declaration*: Modify the signature of a function to better represent its behavior and purpose.

3. *Rename Parameter*: Update the name of a function parameter to better reflect its meaning and usage.

4. *Extract Variable*: Create a new variable to store an intermediate value and improve readability and maintainability. *Extract Constant*: Create a new constant to store a frequently used value and improve code clarity.

5. *Extract Parameter*: Create a new function parameter to increase flexibility and reusability.

6. *Extract Function*: Create a new function to encapsulate a set of related statements and improve modularity.

7. *Slide Statements*: Rearrange the order of statements to improve clarity and readability.

8. *Move Fields*: Move a field from one class to another to better align responsibility and improve maintainability.

9. *Inline Variable*: Remove a redundant or unnecessary variable and simplify the code.

10. *Simplify Logic*: Simplify complex logical expressions to improve clarity and readability.

Let's transform the code together.

Step 1: Slide Statements

Slide Statements is perhaps the simplest refactoring you could find, but sometimes it makes a huge difference. If you imagine arranging source code in a file like arranging things on your desk or ordering books on your bookshelf. Just thinking that *Philosopher's Stone* is between *UNIX Network Programming* and *TCP/IP Guide* on your shelf, what would you do? Yes, slide the *Philosopher's Stone* into its own section.

We see that in the code all the time as well, so Slide Statements is a great technique that can make the code read more smoothly and more coherent.

Just slide the code up and down by pressing `Command+Shift+Up/Down` in WebStorm. You can select multiple lines, a block (a `for-block`, for example), or even a function and then slide them up and down.

```
const letters = "ABCDEFGHIJKLMNOPORSTUVWXYZ";

export const convert = (str: string) => {
  return str.split("")
    .map((c) => {
      const index = letters.indexOf(c);
      if (index !== -1) {
        if (index + 13 >= 26) {
          return letters[index + 13 - 26];
        } else {
          return letters[index + 13];
        }
      }
      return c;
    }).join("");
};
```

Step 2: Extract Constant

It would help if you had a variable whenever you spot an expression that is too long or needs a concept to hold. I'm not treating variables, fields, and constants as different refactorings in JavaScript or TypeScript. The only difference would be the scope of where to put them.

For the following code snippet, the empty string can be extracted as a variable named `separator` as that is what exactly it does. Also, the constant 13 can be pulled into `shift` or `offset` to indicate its meaning (we'll do that in a minute).

Pressing Command+Option+V in WebStorm will do the work:

```
const letters = "ABCDEFGHIJKLMNOPORSTUVWXYZ";
const separator = "";

export const convert = (str: string) => {
  return str.split(separator)
    .map((c) => {
      const index = letters.indexOf(c);
      if (index !== -1) {
        if (index + 13 >= 26) {
          return letters[index + 13 - 26];
        } else {
          return letters[index + 13];
        }
      }
      return c;
    }).join(separator);
};
```

Nothing fancy at all. One important aspect of clean code is it should not raise any surprise to their reader. It should be plain and straightforward.

Step 3: Extract Function

Functions are the most crucial building block in many programming languages, and also it's a perfect place to put your business logic and expressions in. If you don't pay close attention, it can quickly go oversize or have too many things inside.

Although there is no such law for how many lines of code for the function body, I tend to make it small. If it goes too long, I extract a subfunction from some statements to make them readable and easy to modify. *The key here is how you would name your extracted functions.*

For example, the anonymous function inside the map can be extracted into a separate function, which will be much easier to read and test (or be reused in other places).

The shortcut for the Extract Function is Command+Option+M (M for method in object-oriented language).

```
const letters = "ABCDEFGHIJKLMNOPORSTUVWXYZ";
const separator = "";

const transform = (c: string) => {
  const index = letters.indexOf(c);
  if (index !== -1) {
    if (index + 13 >= 26) {
      return letters[index + 13 - 26];
    } else {
      return letters[index + 13];
    }
  }
  return c;
}

export const convert = (str: string) => {
  return str.split(separator)
    .map(transform).join(separator);
};
```

Step 4: Rename Parameter

Renaming a function's parameter is equally as important as renaming a variable inside it. A good parameter name should tell what the expected parameter is for. You may have your own convention here. For example, aLetter is one of the ways I saw a lot in some old codebases. I prefer a generic and short name for parameter names.

Pressing Command+Option+P can start the renaming process in WebStorm. A tiny pop-up will show up, and once you have done the editing, hit Enter to finalize it, and all the references will be updated automatically.

```
const letters = "ABCDEFGHIJKLMNOPORSTUVWXYZ";
const separator = "";

const transform = (letter: string) => {
  const index = letters.indexOf(letter);
  if (index !== -1) {
    if (index + 13 >= 26) {
      return letters[index + 13 - 26];
    } else {
      return letters[index + 13];
    }
  }
  return letter;
}

export const convert = (str: string) => {
  return str.split(separator)
    .map(transform).join(separator);
};
```

Step 5: Rename Variable

The same thing applies to variables as well. There are many times I couldn't think of a good name, then I would use a pretty general one, like x or segment, as a placeholder, and once I made the change and got a better idea of what the variable is holding, I would change the variable name.

```
const dict = "ABCDEFGHIJKLMNOPORSTUVWXYZ";
const separator = "";

const transform = (letter: string) => {
  const index = dict.indexOf(letter);
  if (index !== -1) {
    if (index + 13 >= 26) {
      return dict[index + 13 - 26];
    } else {
      return dict[index + 13];
    }
  }
  return letter;
}

export const convert = (str: string) => {
  return str.split(separator)
    .map(transform).join(separator);
};
```

The old variable `letters` is a bit unclean, so I renamed it to `dict` by pressing Shift+F6. It's a generic renaming shortcut that can also be used for renaming a function.

And since there are quite a few lines in the function `transform`, we can apply the Extract Function one more time.

Step 6: Extract Function

Press Command+Option+M again to extract a new function here called `getLetterWithOffset`. That way, we simplified the `transform` a bit. Note the general principle is that **the smaller a function is, the more likely it can be reused**. We're not aiming for a small function, but reusability is important.

```
const dict = "ABCDEFGHIJKLMNOPORSTUVWXYZ";
const separator = "";

const getLetterWithOffset = (letter: string) => {
  const index = dict.indexOf(letter);

  if (index + 13 >= 26) {
    return dict[index + 13 - 26];
  } else {
    return dict[index + 13];
  }
}

const transform = (letter: string) => {
  const index = dict.indexOf(letter);
  if (index !== -1) {
    return getLetterWithOffset(letter);
  }
  return letter;
}

export const convert = (str: string) => {
  return str.split(separator)
    .map(transform).join(separator);
};
```

Note that a function is the most important building block in most languages, so please pay more attention to the size and meaning of functions. Once you spot an oversized function, try to break it down with Extract Function.

Step 7: Replace `if-else` with `?`

In WebStorm, if you press Option+Enter, some context-related suggestions will pop up. For example, if an `if-else` is short and straightforward enough, I prefer to use a ternary operator to replace them.

```
const dict = "ABCDEFGHIJKLMNOPORSTUVWXYZ";
const separator = "";

const getLetterWithOffset = (letter: string) => {
  const index = dict.indexOf(letter);
  return index + 13 >= 26 ? dict[index + 13 - 26] :
  dict[index + 13];
}

const transform = (letter: string) => {
  const index = dict.indexOf(letter);
  if (index !== -1) {
    return getLetterWithOffset(letter);
  }
  return letter;
}

export const convert = (str: string) => {
  return str.split(separator)
    .map(transform).join(separator);
};
```

In WebStorm, Option+Enter often gives you great options when you are not sure what to optimize. I also use it to fix the auto import when it complains that some constants, types, or functions are not defined or to fix incompatible type issues.

Step 8: Extract Function

Let's do the Extract Function one more time by pressing Command+Option+M to put the index calculation out as a separate function. It seems there is some pattern about to emerge once we have the getIndex, isn't it?

```
const dict = "ABCDEFGHIJKLMNOPQRSTUVWXYZ";
const separator = "";

const getIndex = (index: number) => {
  return index + 13 >= 26 ? index + 13 - 26 : index + 13;
}

const getLetterWithOffset = (letter: string) => {
  const index = dict.indexOf(letter);
  return dict[getIndex(index)];
}

const transform = (letter: string) => {
  const index = dict.indexOf(letter);
  if (index !== -1) {
    return getLetterWithOffset(letter);
  }
  return letter;
}

export const convert = (str: string) => {
  return str.split(separator)
    .map(transform).join(separator);
};
```

Even in some cases, it may seem unnecessary to create a new function, but it is worth doing it as, in many cases, once you extract a new one, some duplications would appear like magic. And the worst case is that you can always inline the extracted logic back by pressing Command+Option+N in WebStorm.

Step 9: Extract Parameter

Extract Parameter often happens during a big refactoring inside a function. When you need an internal state to be passed in from the outside world, and you don't want to use a global constant at that point, you can extract a parameter first and then in the calling place, pass in a variable (could be a global constant).

```
const dict = "ABCDEFGHIJKLMNOPQRSTUVWXYZ";
const separator = "";

const getIndex = (index: number, offset: number) => {
  return index + offset >= 26 ? index + offset - 26 : index
  + offset;
}

const getLetterWithOffset = (letter: string) => {
  const index = dict.indexOf(letter);
  return dict[getIndex(index, 13)];
}

const transform = (letter: string) => {
  const index = dict.indexOf(letter);
  if (index !== -1) {
    return getLetterWithOffset(letter);
  }
  return letter;
}

export const convert = (str: string) => {
  return str.split(separator)
    .map(transform).join(separator);
};
```

Here, we extract an optional parameter with Command+Option+P first with a default value, so it will not break any existing code. Then we can check all the call sites and fix them.

Step 10: Extract Constant

It seems the 13 here is not really meaningful, so let's use Command+Option+C to give it a better name. Note you can use a family of keyboard shortcuts to extract constant (Command+Option+C), extract variable (Command+Option+V), extract parameter (Command+Option+P), and extract method (function) (Command+Option+M).

```
const dict = "ABCDEFGHIJKLMNOPQRSTUVWXYZ";
const separator = "";

const getIndex = (index: number, offset: number) => {
  return index + offset >= 26 ? index + offset - 26 : index
  + offset;
}

const getLetterWithOffset = (letter: string) => {
  const index = dict.indexOf(letter);
  const shift = 13;
  return dict[getIndex(index, shift)];
}

const transform = (letter: string) => {
  const index = dict.indexOf(letter);
  if (index !== -1) {
    return getLetterWithOffset(letter);
  }
  return letter;
}
```

```
export const convert = (str: string) => {
  return str.split(separator)
    .map(transform).join(separator);
};
```

Step 11: Slide Statements

We then would slide this constant up to the variable definition area for the next move:

```
const dict = "ABCDEFGHIJKLMNOPQRSTUVWXYZ";
const separator = "";
const shift = 13;

const getIndex = (index: number, offset: number) => {
  return index + offset >= 26 ? index + offset - 26 : index
  + offset;
}

const getLetterWithOffset = (letter: string) => {
  const index = dict.indexOf(letter);
  return dict[getIndex(index, shift)];
}

const transform = (letter: string) => {
  const index = dict.indexOf(letter);
  if (index !== -1) {
    return getLetterWithOffset(letter);
  }
  return letter;
}
```

```
export const convert = (str: string) => {
  return str.split(separator)
    .map(transform).join(separator);
};
```

As we mentioned earlier, you not only can slide one statement but also a couple of statements, a block, or a function. Select the block and press Command+Shift+Up/Down.

Step 12: Move Fields

Often when you slide statements up to the higher scope or extract a few utility functions, you will soon realize it may be good to move them into a place so other modules can use them. Also, I found even if it's not that commonly reusable, moving them to a separate file can make the current file concise, thus easier to read and understand.

Pressing F6 will launch a pop-up for you; then select variables and functions that you would like to move out, type in a file name, and you're done. If the file doesn't exist, WebStorm will create one for you. Otherwise, the content will be amended.

Let's say we would like to move

```
export const dict = "ABCDEFGHIJKLMNOPQRSTUVWXYZ";
export const separator = "";
export const shift = 13;
```

into file constants.ts, and then in file convert.ts, we reference these constants:

```
import {dict, separator, shift} from "./constants";

const getIndex = (index: number, offset: number) => {
  return index + offset >= 26 ? index + offset - 26 : index
  + offset;
}
```

```
const getLetterWithOffset = (letter: string) => {
  const index = dict.indexOf(letter);
  return dict[getIndex(index, shift)];
}

const transform = (letter: string) => {
  const index = dict.indexOf(letter);
  if (index !== -1) {
    return getLetterWithOffset(letter);
  }
  return letter;
}

export const convert = (str: string) => {
  return str.split(separator)
    .map(transform).join(separator);
};
```

Step 13: Function to Arrow Function

The arrow function should be your default choice now. It's more compact and clear once you get used to it. I only use the traditional function declaration (with function keyword) in very few cases, like a React function name that displayName matters.

```
import {dict, separator, shift} from "./constants";

const getIndex = (index: number, offset: number) => {
  return index + offset >= 26 ? index + offset - 26 : index
  + offset;
}
```

```
const getLetterWithOffset = (letter: string) => {
  const index = dict.indexOf(letter);
  return dict[getIndex(index, shift)];
}

const transform = (letter: string) => {
  if (dict.indexOf(letter) !== -1) {
    return getLetterWithOffset(letter);
  }
  return letter;
}

export const convert = (str: string) => {
  return str.split(separator)
    .map(transform).join(separator);
};
```

This can be done by Option+Enter. WebStorm will show you a couple of great suggestions. And in this case, **convert to variable holding arrow function** would do the work.

Step 14: Simplify Logic

Finally, let's make some final touches to make the code look even more professional.

For example:

- Simplify the one statement arrow function.

- Use dict.includes to replace dict.indexOf.

- Use dict.length to replace hardcode 26.

- Use mod operation % to get a new index when it is out of dict bound.

```
import {dict, separator, shift} from "./constants";

const getIndex = (index: number, offset: number) =>
  (index + offset) % dict. length;

const getLetterWithOffset = (letter: string) => {
  const index = dict.indexOf(letter);
  return dict[getIndex(index, shift)];
}

const transform = (letter: string) =>
  dict.includes(letter) ? getLetterWithOffset(letter) : letter

export const convert = (str: string) =>
  str.split(separator)
    .map(transform).join(separator);
```

And when we run all the tests again, it should not surprise us at all.

Summary

To recap, this chapter provided a step-by-step guide on using keyboard shortcuts (in WebStorm IDE) to simplify your code and make it easier to modify. By mastering these essential refactorings, you can improve your coding efficiency and productivity. Don't hesitate to revisit this chapter as needed, and feel free to move on to the next chapter to continue building on your coding skills.

CHAPTER 4

Test-Driven Development Essentials

In this chapter, we will learn how to apply TDD in your daily development routine through a step-by-step guide. Along with this demo, you will get an idea of how to split a big task into relatively smaller ones and complete each one with a set of passing tests while learning some refactoring techniques. Before we dive into the code, let's get a fundamental understanding of how to write a proper test.

Writing Tests

So how would you start to write a test? Typically, there are three steps (as always, even to put an elephant into a fridge) required. Firstly, do some preparation work, like setting up the database, initializing the object to be tested, or loading some fixture data. Secondly, invoke the method or function to be tested, usually assigning the result to some variable. Finally, do some assertions to see whether the result is as expected or not.

© Juntao Qiu 2023
J. Qiu, *Test-Driven Development with React and TypeScript*,
https://doi.org/10.1007/978-1-4842-9648-6_4

Using Given-When-Then to Arrange a Test

Given-When-Then (GWT) is a common and effective structure for writing tests in software development. The GWT structure provides a clear and concise way to organize and document tests, and it helps ensure that tests are comprehensive, covering all possible scenarios and edge cases.

It consists of three essential components of a test:

1. *Given*: The initial context or setup for the test. This includes any data or objects that need to be created or initialized before the test can be executed.

2. *When*: The action or behavior being tested. This is the part of the test where a specific action or operation is performed on the given context.

3. *Then*: The expected outcome or result of the test. This is where the expected behavior or state of the system is defined, and the actual result is compared to the expected result.

By breaking down a test into these three components, the GWT structure can help ensure that tests are clear, well organized, and easy to understand. It also helps to ensure that tests are comprehensive, covering all possible scenarios and edge cases.

A test can also be described in 3A format; the 3A (Arrange-Act-Assert) structure consists of three essential components of a test:

1. *Arrange*: The initial context or setup for the test

2. *Act*: The action or behavior being tested

3. *Assert*: The expected outcome or result of the test

They are essentially the same thing. Let's take the GWT as an example here.

As an example, say we have the following snippet:

```
// given
const user = User.create({
  name: "Juntao",
  address: "ThoughtWorks Software Technologies (Melbourne)",
});

// when
const name = user.getName();
const address = user.getAddress();

// then
expect(name).toEqual("Juntao");
expect(address).toEqual("ThoughtWorks Software Technologies
(Melbourne)");
```

Typically, you will split test cases with many assertions into several independent ones and let each have a single assertion, like so:

```
it("creates user name", () => {
  // given
  const user = User.create({
    name: "Juntao",
    address: "ThoughtWorks Software Technologies (Melbourne)",
  });

  // when
  const name = user.getName();

  // then
  expect(name).toEqual("Juntao");
});
```

```
it("creates user address", () => {
  // given
  const user = User.create({
    name: "Juntao",
    address: "ThoughtWorks Software Technologies (Melbourne)",
  });

  // when
  const address = user.getAddress();

  // then
  expect(address).toEqual("ThoughtWorks Software Technologies
  (Melbourne)");
});
```

Please note there is some debate among developers about whether each test case should have only one assertion or multiple assertions.

Advocates of the "one assertion per test case" approach argue that it helps make tests more focused and specific, making it easier to identify the cause of a test failure. When a test case has multiple assertions, it can be more difficult to determine which assertion caused the test to fail, potentially slowing down the debugging process.

On the other hand, supporters of the "multiple assertions per test case" approach argue that it can lead to more efficient and effective testing, as it allows multiple aspects of the code to be tested with a single test case. This can also help reduce duplication in test cases and make testing more maintainable.

Ultimately, the choice of whether to use one assertion or multiple assertions per test case will depend on the specific requirements and constraints of the project, as well as personal preferences and team standards. Regardless of which approach is used, the important thing is to ensure that tests are well designed, comprehensive, and effective in catching errors and bugs.

Triangulation Method

In Test-Driven Development (TDD), `triangulation` is a technique used to help guide the creation of tests.

This method involves writing a test for a specific behavior, running the test, and then writing another test that forces the code to behave in a different way. By iteratively writing tests that explore different paths or scenarios, the developer can gain a deeper understanding of the requirements and constraints of the code and can create more robust and comprehensive tests.

Imagine we are implementing a calculator with TDD. A test for `addition` could be a good starting point.

Example: Function `addition`

The First Test for `addition`

The specification of `addition` could be

```
describe('addition', () => {
  it('returns 5 when adding 2 and 3', () => {
    const a: number = 2;
    const b: number = 3;

    const result: number = add(a, b);

    expect(result).toEqual(5);
  });
});
```

A Quick and Dirty Implementation

The simplest implementation to make the test pass can be

```
const add = () => 5
```

At first glance, it might seem very strange to write your function like this. But it has several benefits. For example, it's a good way for a developer to verify if everything is connected correctly. It drives the creation of the add function and the data type of the function.

A typical technique to check if your tests are actually linked to the code is to make an obvious failure. For example, run the preceding test to see it pass, and then modify the preceding value 5 to 3 to see if the test is still passing. When test and implementation are not linked properly, you can get a misleading *green* test.

The Second Test Case to Make Our Implementation Less Specific

Now let's create another test for the add function:

```
it('returns 6 when adding 2 and 4', () => {
  const a: number = 2;
  const b: number = 4;

  const result: number = add(a, b);

  expect(result).toEqual(6);
});
```

To make the test pass, the simplest solution then becomes

```
const add = (a: number, b: number): number => 2 + b;
```

The idea is to write a failing but specific test to drive the implementation code to be more generic, in each step. So now the implementation is more generic than in the first step. However, there's still some room for improvement.

The Final and Simple Implementation

The third test could be something like

```
it("returns 7 when adding 3 and 4", () => {
  const a: number = 3;
  const b: number = 4;

  const result: number = add(a, b);

  expect(result).toEqual(7);
});
```

This time, there are no patterns in the test data to follow, so we have to write something more complicated to make it pass. The implementation becomes

```
const add = (a: number, b: number): number => a + b;
```

Now the implementation is more generic and will cover most `addition` scenarios. In the future, our calculator might need to support `addition` for imaginary numbers; we can do that by adding more tests to drive out the solution in the same way.

And now you see why the approach is called `Triangulation`: you write a failed test and write just *enough* code to make the test pass, then you write another test to drive the changes from another angle. And that, in turn, will lead you to make the implementation more generic. You continue working in this manner, step by step, until the code becomes generic enough to support most of the cases that fall within the business requirements.

While it may appear to be a simplistic and time-consuming approach, this baby step method provides a solid foundation for software development that you can and should depend on. Whether you're tackling simple tasks or complex projects, the same fundamental process applies. This is because TDD emphasizes breaking down larger tasks into smaller, more manageable pieces, making the overall process more manageable and less daunting. By adopting this approach, you can simplify tasks and ensure that your code is well tested and robust.

OK, let's move one step further by looking into applying TDD in a more complicated example.

How to Do Tasking with TDD

In Test-Driven Development, tasking refers to the process of breaking down a larger problem into smaller, more manageable tasks. By breaking the problem down into smaller pieces, it becomes easier to identify and solve specific issues, and the overall development process becomes more manageable and less daunting.

Tasking involves defining specific tasks or subtasks that need to be completed in order to achieve the desired outcome. Each task should be well defined, clearly outlined, and achievable within a specific timeframe. By focusing on completing each task one at a time, developers can gradually build up the functionality of their codebase and ensure that each component is well tested and functioning as expected.

The tasking process can also help identify potential issues or roadblocks early on in the development process, allowing developers to adjust their approach and refine their strategy accordingly. Overall, tasking is an important aspect of TDD and can help ensure that the development process is well organized, efficient, and effective.

In the project I'm currently working on, our team uses a very simple manner to track the efforts put into each user story (a small chunk of work that could be accomplished independently). Usually, a card can have one of the following statuses: analysis, doing, testing, or done, as it progresses through its lifecycle. If a user story cannot progress because it depends on something that is incomplete or not yet ready, we mark it as blocked. This system allows us to easily track the progress of each user story and identify any potential issues or roadblocks in the development process.

The measure of efforts on stories we're using is pretty simple. Basically, we track how many days were spent on coding or how many days it was blocked. The project manager then has a chance to understand what progress looks like and what the overall health status of the project is and maybe any further actions that could be taken to improve it.

We put a d in lowercase in the title of a card to indicate that it has been under development for half a day and an uppercase D for a full day. Not surprisingly, q is for half a QA day and Q for a whole QA day. This means that at any given moment, you will see something like this on the title of a card: [ddDQbq] Allow user to login to their profile page – the b is for blocked.

An Expression Parser for Tracking Progress

Let's build a parser that can read the tracking marks ddDQbq and translate it into a human-readable format, something like this:

```
{
  "Dev days": 2.0,
  "QA days": 1,
  "Blocked": 0.5
}
```

Looks pretty straightforward, right? Can't wait to jump in and write the code? Hold on, let's get started with a test first, and get a feeling of how to apply TDD in such a case.

Split the Parser to Subtasks

So the first question could be **how can we split a task like this into smaller tasks that are easy to achieve and verify?** While there are multiple ways to do it, a reasonable split could be

1. Write a test to make sure we can translate d to half a dev day.

2. Write a test to make sure we can translate D to one dev day.

3. Write a test to handle more than one mark like dD.

4. Write a test to handle q.

5. Write a test to handle qQ.

6. Write a test to handle ddQ.

As we discussed in Chapter 1, the splitting is essential for applying TDD. And small tasks should be engaging and encourage you in different ways:

1. It's fun (it has been proven that when we experience small amounts of achievement, our brains release dopamine, which is connected to feelings of pleasure, learning, and motivation).

2. It ensures fast feedback.

3. It allows you to easily understand the progress of the task at any given time.

Applying TDD Step by Step
The First Test – Parse and Calculate Mark d

OK, enough theory, let's get our hands dirty. According to the output of the tasking step, the first test should be

```
it("translates d to half a dev day", () => {
  expect(translate("d")).toEqual({ Dev: 0.5 });
});
```

And pretty straightforwardly, the implementation could be as simple as

```
const translate = () => ({ Dev: 0.5 });
```

It ignores the input and returns a dummy {'Dev': 0.5}, but you have to admire that it fulfills the requirement regarding the current subtask. Quick and dirty, but it works.

The Second Test – For Mark D

Let's cross off the first to-do from our task list and move on:

```
it("translates D to one dev day", () => {
  expect(translate("D")).toEqual({ Dev: 1.0 });
});
```

What's the most straightforward solution you can think of? Maybe something like this:

```
const translate = (c: string) => (c === "d" ? { Dev: 0.5 } :
{ Dev: 1.0 });
```

I know it seems silly to write code in this way. However, as you can see, our implementation is driven by the related tests. As long as the tests pass – which means the requirements are met – we could call it satisfied. After all, the only reason we write code is to fulfill some business requirement, right?

As the tests are now passing, you can do some refactoring if you find something could be improved, for example, magic numbers, or the method body is too long. For now, I think we're OK to continue.

The Combination of Notes d and D

The third test could be

```
it("translates dD to one and a half dev days", () => {
  expect(translate("dD")).toEqual({ Dev: 1.5 });
});
```

Hmm, things become more complicated now; we have to parse the string of characters individually and sum up the result. The following code snippet should do the trick:

```
const translate = (input: string) => {
  let sum: number = 0;

  input.split("").forEach((c: string) => (sum += c === "d" ?
  0.5 : 1.0));

  return { Dev: sum };
};
```

Now our program can handle all the d or D combination sequences like ddd or DDdDd without a problem. Then comes task four:

```
it("translates q to half a qa day", () => {
  expect(translate("q")).toEqual({ QA: 0.5 });
});
```

It seems we need a sum function for each status, for example, sum in Dev, sum in QA. It would be more convenient if we can refactor the code a little to make that change easier. And thus, the most beautiful part of TDD emerges – you don't have to worry about breaking any of the existing functionalities by accident since you have the tests to cover them.

Refactoring – Extract Functions

Let's extract the parsing part out as a function itself and use that function in translate.

The translate function could then be something like this after the refactoring:

```
const parse = (c: string) => {
  switch(c) {
    case 'd': return {status: 'Dev', effort: 0.5};
    case 'D': return {status: 'Dev', effort: 1};
  }
};

const translate = (input: string) => {
  const state: {[key: string]: number} = {
    'Dev': 0,
    'QA': 0
  };

  input.split('').forEach((c: string) => {
    const {status, effort} = parse(c);
    state[status] = state[status] + effort;
  });

  return state;
};
```

Now it should be effortless to make the new test pass. We can add one new case in parse:

```
const parse = (c: string) => {
  switch (c) {
    case "d":
      return { status: "Dev", effort: 0.5 };
```

```
    case "D":
      return { status: "Dev", effort: 1 };
    case "q":
      return { status: "QA", effort: 0.5 };
  }
};
```

Keep Refactoring – Extract Functions to Files

For the task that contains different characters, there is no change required in the code at all. However, as a responsible programmer, we could keep cleaning the code up to an *ideal* status. For example, we could extract the parse to a lookup dictionary:

```
const dict = {
  d: {
    status: "Dev",
    effort: 0.5,
  },
  D: {
    status: "Dev",
    effort: 1.0,
  },
  q: {
    status: "QA",
    effort: 0.5,
  },
  Q: {
    status: "QA",
    effort: 1.0,
  },
};
```

and that would simplify the parse function to something like

```
const parse = (c: string) => dict[c];
```

You can even extract the dict as data into a separate file named constants and import it into translator.js for the sake of clarity. For the forEach function in translate, we could use Array.reduce to make it even shorter:

```
const translate = (input: string) => {
  const items = input.split("");
  return items.reduce((accumulator, current) => {
    const { status, effort } = parse(current);
    accumulator[status] = (accumulator[status] || 0) + effort;
    return accumulator;
  }, {});
};
```

As we can see from the test cases in Figure 4-1, our translator code is now passing all tests and is both nice and clean.

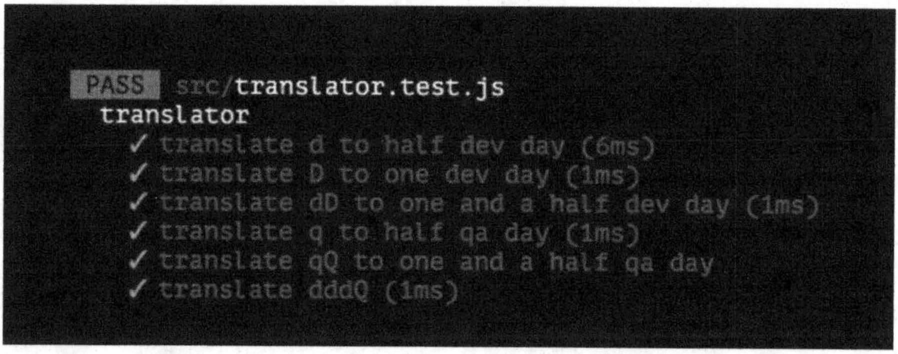

Figure 4-1. *All test cases for translator are passing*

It's important to note that the refactoring process can be an ongoing one, and you should continue to refactor until you feel comfortable with the code. However, be careful not to overengineer the code by making too many assumptions about potential changes or abstracting the code to a level beyond what is actually helpful.

Summary

In this chapter, we have learned about the three fundamental steps of effective test writing and discovered how to use `Triangulation` to explore various paths in our tests. We also familiarized ourselves with `tasking` as a way to structure our test writing process. We then applied these concepts to a small program and followed the TDD methodology step by step. As a result, we've developed a practical understanding of how TDD can lead to the creation of more robust and maintainable code, even in complex projects.

CHAPTER 5

Project Setup

Before delving into the core content of this book, it is crucial to establish the necessary infrastructures. In this chapter, we will focus on setting up key components to lay the groundwork for our project. Firstly, we will create the project codebase and skeleton structure using `create-react-app`. Next, we will incorporate the `Material UI` framework to streamline the development of the user interface. Lastly, we will configure the `Cypress` end-to-end UI testing framework.

These setups are essential to ensure a solid foundation for our subsequent discussions and enable efficient development and testing processes. Let's begin by establishing these fundamental infrastructures and set ourselves up for success in the chapters ahead.

Application Requirements

In this book, we are going to develop a web application from scratch. We will call it `Bookish`; it's a simple application about `books` – as the name implies. In the application, a user could have a book list and can search books by keywords, and users are allowed to navigate to a book detail page and review the `description`, `review`, and `ranking` of the book. We will complete some of the features in an iterative manner, applying ATDD (Acceptance Test-Driven Development) along the way.

In the application, we will develop several typical features including the book list and book detail pages, as well as the searching and reviewing functionalities.

© Juntao Qiu 2023
J. Qiu, *Test-Driven Development with React and TypeScript*,
https://doi.org/10.1007/978-1-4842-9648-6_5

Feature 1 – Book List

In the real world, the granularity of a feature would be much bigger than the ones we're describing in this book. Typically, there would be many user stories within a feature, such as a book list, pagination, the styling of the book list, and so on. Let's assume there is only one story per feature here.

We can describe the user story in this form:

> As a user I want to see a list of books So that I can learn something new

This format for describing a user story is widely used and has several advantages. By beginning with "As a ", it emphasizes the user who would benefit from the feature, while "I want to " explains how they will interact with the system. The final sentence, "So that ", describes the business value of the feature.

By following this format, we are compelled to view the story from the stakeholder's perspective and to convey to both business analysts and developers the most important and valuable aspect of the user story.

The acceptance criteria are

- Given there are 10 books in the system, a user should see 10 items on the page.

- In each item, the following information should be displayed: book name, author, price, rating.

Acceptance criteria can sometimes be written in the following format:

```
Given there are `10` books in the library
When a user visits the homepage
Then he/she would see `10` books on the page
And each book would contain at least `name`, `author`, `price`
and `rating`
```

The given clause explains the current status of the application; when means the user triggers some action, for example, clicks a button or navigates to a page; and then is an assertion that states the expected performance of the application.

Feature 2 – Book Detail

Our second feature would be to implement the book detail page:

> As a user I want to see the details of a book So that I can quickly get an understanding of what it's about

And the acceptance criteria are

- A user clicks an item in the book list and is redirected to the detail page.

- The detail page displays the book name, author, price, description, and any reviews.

Feature 3 – Searching

The third feature is to implement searching by name; it can be described as follows:

> As a user I want to search for a book by its name So that I can quickly find what I'm interested in

And the acceptance criteria are

- The user types Refactoring as a search word.

- Only books with Refactoring in their name are displayed in the book list.

Feature 4 – Book Reviews

And then we need to show review information besides the other sections on the detail page:

> As a user I want to be able to add a review to a book I have read previously So that people who have the same interests could decide if it is worthwhile to read

And the corresponding acceptance criteria are

- A user can read the reviews on the detail page.

- A user can post a review to a particular book.

- A user can edit the review they have posted.

With all those requirements well defined, we can start with project setting up.

Create the Project

Let's get started with some essential package installation and configuration first. Make sure you have node (at least node >= 8.10 and npm >= 5.6 are required) installed locally. After that, you can use npm to install the tools we need to build our Bookish application (we have already covered that part in the previous chapter, check it out in case you haven't).

Using `create-react-app`

After the installation is complete, we can use the `create-react-app` package to create our project:

```
npx create-react-app bookish-react --template typescript
```

create-react-app will install react, react-dom, and a command-line tool named react-scripts by default. Moreover, it will download those libraries and their dependencies automatically, including webpack, babel, and others. By using create-react-app, we don't need any config to get the application up and running.

After the creation process, as the console log suggests, we can jump into the bookish-react folder and run npm start and you should be able to see a screen like Figure 5-1

```
cd bookish-react
npm start
```

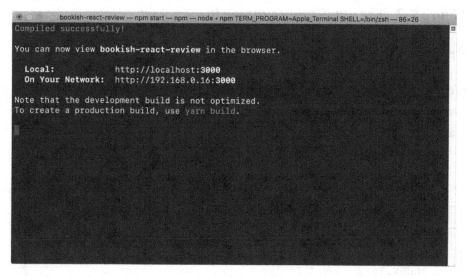

Figure 5-1. *Launching your application in the terminal*

There will be a new browser tab opened automatically at this address: http://localhost:3000. And the UI should look like Figure 5-2.

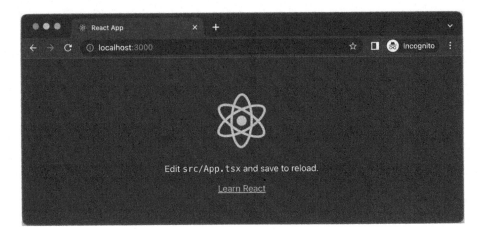

Figure 5-2. *The application running in a browser*

Project File Structure

We don't need all of the files generated by create-react-app, so let's do some cleanup first. We can remove all the irrelevant files in the src folder, leaving us with the following files:

```
src
├── App.css
├── App.test.tsx
├── App.tsx
├── index.css
├── index.tsx
└── setupTests.ts
```

Modify the App.tsx file content so it looks as follows:

```
import React from 'react';
import './App.css';

function App() {
  return (
```

```
    <div className='App'>
      <h1>Hello world</h1>
    </div>
  );
}
```

```
export default App;
```

and the `index.tsx` like this:

```tsx
import React from 'react';
import ReactDOM from 'react-dom/client';
import './index.css';
import App from './App';

const root = ReactDOM.createRoot(
  document.getElementById('root') as HTMLElement
);

root.render(<App />);
```

Then our UI should look something like Figure 5-3.

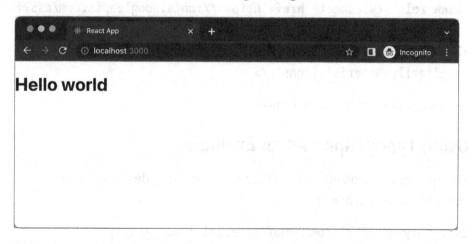

Figure 5-3. *After cleanup*

Material UI Library

To make the application we're demonstrating here look more realistic, as well as reduce the css tricks in the code snippets, we will use Material UI. Material UI is a library of React UI components that implements Google's Material Design.

It contains many reusable components that are ready to be used out of the box, such as Tabs, ExpandablePanel, and others. It will help us to build our bookish app faster and more easily.

The installation is pretty straightforward; another npm install will do:

```
npm install @mui/material @emotion/react @emotion/styled @mui/
icons-material --save
```

After that, let's put some fonts in our public/index.html to improve the look and feel.

Font and Icons

Note the second line is for svg icons:

```
<link rel='stylesheet' href='https://fonts.googleapis.com/css?f
amily=Roboto:300,400,500,700&display=swap' />
<link rel='stylesheet' href='https://fonts.googleapis.com/
icon?family=Material+Icons' />
```

That's all what we need for now.

Using Typography As an Example

We can use a Component from Material UI in our code, importing the module like this in App.js:

```
import Typography from '@mui/material/Typography';
```

And then change the h1 to <Typography>:

```
function App() {
  return (
    <Typography variant='h2' component='h2' data-
    test='heading'>
      Bookish
    </Typography>
  );
}
```

By using Material UI, we don't need a separate file for css anymore, as it utilizes the css-in-js approach to make the component encapsulated and independent. We can then remove all the .css files, making sure to also remove any references to them.

Now the project structure has just two files left:

```
src
├── App.tsx
└── index.tsx
```

index.tsx should look like this:

```
import React from 'react';
import ReactDOM from 'react-dom/client';
import './index.css';
import App from './App';

const root = ReactDOM.createRoot(
  document.getElementById('root') as HTMLElement
);

root.render(<App />);
```

and App.tsx like this:

```
import React from "react";
import Typography from "@mui/material/Typography";

function App() {
  return (
    <Typography variant="h2" component="h2" data-
    test="heading">
      Bookish
    </Typography>
  );
}

export default App;
```

All right, now we have the basic application set up. You should be able to see the result on your browser like Figure 5-4.

Figure 5-4. *Launch the application in a browser*

And next, let's install the end-to-end testing framework we're going to use in the rest of the book.

Install Cypress

In the first edition of this book, I used puppeteer as the engine for UI functional tests, and it's a great tool for that purpose. However, I found its API is too low level from most beginners. From the end-user perspective, you have to remember a lot of unnecessary details such as async/await pairs when querying elements on the page. And it does not provide basic helpers, such as fixtures or stubs, which are widely used in TDD.

So this time, I will use Cypress instead – the idea is pretty much the same; Cypress gives us more options and better mechanisms to reduce the effort of writing tests. Features such as fixture and route are shipped with the tool that can make our life much easier.

The good news is that installation is simple, and you don't have to configure it at all.

Set Up Cypress

Let's run the following command to start:

```
npm install cypress --save-dev
```

After the installation, make sure the app is running, and then we can run the cypress command to launch the GUI (as shown in Figure 5-5) to create our first test suite:

```
npx cypress open
```

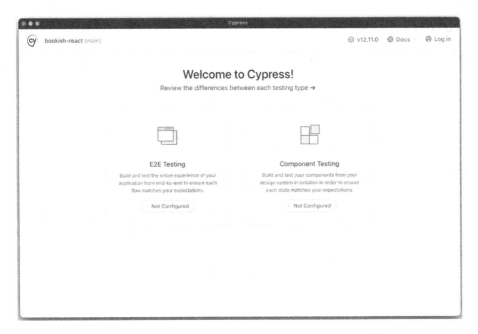

Figure 5-5. *Launch cypress from the terminal*

This will create a new folder called cypress outside of our project code. Following the cypress configure wizard, we can create a new specification file (just a fancy word for test file here), called bookish.spec.cy.ts. The file will be under the cypress/e2e folder under our project:

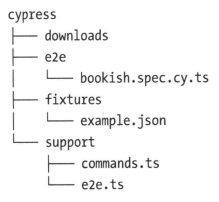

```
cypress
├── downloads
├── e2e
│   └── bookish.spec.cy.ts
├── fixtures
│   └── example.json
└── support
    ├── commands.ts
    └── e2e.ts
```

For now, the only thing we need to care about is bookish.spec.cy.ts. We will examine fixtures in the coming chapters.

Our First End-to-End Test

Do you remember when we talked about how the most challenging part of TDD might be where to start and how to write the very first test?

A feasible option for our first test could be

- Make sure there is a Heading element on the page, and the content is Bookish.

This test might look like pointless at first glance, but actually it can make sure that

- Frontend code can compile and translate.

- The browser can render our page correctly (without any script errors).

So, in our bookish.spec.cy.ts, simply put

```
describe('Bookish application', function() {
  it('Visits the bookish', function() {
    cy.visit('http://localhost:3000/');
    cy.get('h2[data-test="heading"]').contains('Bookish')
  })
})
```

cy is the global object in cypress. It contains almost everything we need to write tests: navigating to the browser, querying an element on the page, and doing the assertions. The test we just wrote is trying to visit http://localhost:3000/, and then make sure the h2 with the data-test attribute as heading has content equal to the string: Bookish (Figure 5-6).

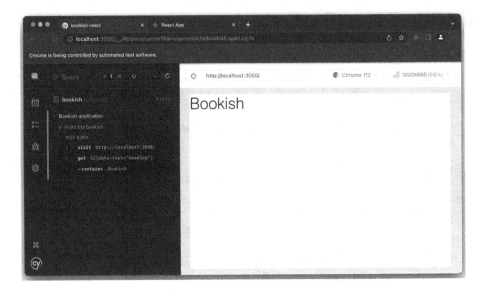

Figure 5-6. *Our first end-to-end test in Cypress*

In the daily development workflow, especially when there are several end-to-end tests running, you might not want to see all the details (fill out form fields, scroll the pages, or some notifications), so you can configure it to run in headless mode:

```
npx cypress run
```

Define a Shortcut Command

Just define a new task under the scripts section in package.json:

```
"scripts": {
  "start": "react-scripts start",
  "build": "react-scripts build",
  "test": "react-scripts test",
  "eject": "react-scripts eject",
  "e2e": "cypress run"
},
```

Make sure the app is running (`npm start`), then run `npm run e2e` from another terminal. This will do all the dirty work for you and give you a detailed report after all tests are complete.

Commit Code to Version Control

Beautiful! We now have an acceptance test and its corresponding implementation, and we can commit the code to version control just in case we need to look back in the future. I'm going to use `git` in this book since it's the most popular one and you will find it installed in almost every developer's computer nowadays.

Running the following command will initialize the current folder as a `git` repository:

```
git init
```

Then commit it locally. Of course, you may want to also push it to some remote repository like GitHub or GitLab to share it with colleagues:

```
git add .
git commit -m "make the first e2e test pass"
```

Files to Ignore

If you have something you don't want to be published or shared with others, create a `.gitignore` text file in the root directory, and put the file name you don't want to be shared in it, like so:

```
*.log
.idea/
debug/
```

The preceding list will ignore any files with `log` extension and folder `.idea` (it's autogenerated by JetBrains IDEs like WebStorm).

Summary

In this chapter, we made significant progress in setting up our project and conducting our first end-to-end test. Using `create-react-app`, we established the initial project structure, providing a solid foundation for development. To enhance the user interface, we integrated `Material UI` and leveraged its customizable components.

We introduced and configured `Cypress`, a powerful testing tool, allowing us to conduct end-to-end tests. Taking the first step, we created our inaugural end-to-end test, verifying the application's functionality.

These achievements establish a robust testing framework and lay the groundwork for further development. With project setup complete, Material UI integrated, and an initial end-to-end test executed successfully, we're ready to focus on implementing core functionality.

Building upon this foundation, we'll tackle upcoming challenges with confidence. Our solid project structure and testing capabilities ensure we can create a healthy application, meeting the desired features.

Implement the Book List

Our first requirement is to implement a book list. From the perspective of the acceptance tests, all we have to do is to make sure that the page contains a list of books – we don't need to worry about what technology will be used to implement the page. And it doesn't matter if the page is dynamically generated or just static HTML, as long as there is a list of books on the page.

Taking baby steps is crucial at this stage. Initially, we can fake the functionality to make the acceptance tests pass and then gradually replace the static content with dynamic code.

Acceptance Tests for Book List

A List (of Books)

First things first, let's add a test case in `bookish.spec.js` within the `describe` block:

```
it('Shows a book list', () => {
  cy.visit('http://localhost:3000/');
  cy.get('div[data-test="book-list"]').should('exist');
  cy.get('div.book-item').should('have.length', 2);
})
```

© Juntao Qiu 2023
J. Qiu, *Test-Driven Development with React and TypeScript*,
https://doi.org/10.1007/978-1-4842-9648-6_6

We expect that there is a container that has the `data-test` attribute of `book-list` and that this container has several `.book-item` elements. If we run the test now (`npm run e2e`), it will fail miserably, as shown in Figure 6-1.

Figure 6-1. *Failed end-to-end test*

Following the steps of TDD, we need to implement the simplest possible code to make the test pass. We can add the HTML structure of the book into `App.tsx`:

```
function App() {
  return (
    <>
      <Typography variant="h2" component="h2" data-
      test="heading">
        Bookish
      </Typography>
      <div data-test="book-list">
        <div className="book-item"></div>
```

```
      <div className="book-item"></div>
    </div>
  </>
  );
}
```

Excellent, the test has passed successfully. As a result, we have driven the HTML structure through the test, which is a great accomplishment. Note that we hard-coded two book-item divs inside a container div.

Verify Book Name

Let's move on to the next step and add another expectation to the test:

```
it('Shows a book list', () => {
  cy.visit('http://localhost:3000/');

  cy.get('div[data-test="book-list"]').should('exist');
  cy.get('div.book-item').should((books) => {
    expect(books).to.have.length(2);

    const titles = [...books].map(x => x.querySelector('h2').
    innerHTML);
    expect(titles).to.deep.equal(
      ['Refactoring', 'Domain-driven design']
    )
  })
})
```

To make this test pass, we can again hard-code the HTML we expect in App.tsx:

```
<div data-test='book-list'>
  <div className='book-item'>
    <h2 className='title'>Refactoring</h2>
```

```
  </div>
  <div className='book-item'>
    <h2 className='title'>Domain-driven design</h2>
  </div>
</div>
```

Awesome! Our tests pass again (Figure 6-2).

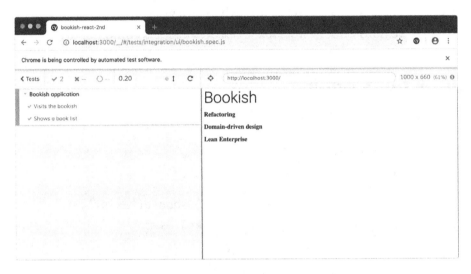

Figure 6-2. *UI tests are now passing*

Now it's time to review the code to check if there are any code smells and then undertake any necessary refactoring.

Refactoring – Extract Function

Firstly, putting all the .book-item elements in the render method might not be ideal. Instead, we can use a for loop to generate the HTML content.

As developers who strive for clean code, we understand that static repetition is undesirable. To address this, we can extract the repetitive portion as a variable called books and utilize the map function instead. This approach allows for more efficient and concise code, promoting maintainability and readability.

```
 Function App() {
+  const books = [{ name: 'Refactoring' }, { name: 'Domain-
driven design' }];
+

   return (
     <div>
       <Typography variant='h2' component='h2' data-
       test='heading'>
       Bookish
       </Typography>
       <div data-test='book-list'>
-        <div className='book-item'>
-          <h2 className='title'>Refactoring</h2>
-        </div>
-        <div className='book-item'>
-          <h2 className='title'>Domain-driven design</h2>
-        </div>
+        {
+          books.map(book => (<div className='book-item'>
+            <h2 className='title'>{book.name}</h2>
+          </div>))
+        }
       </div>
     </div>
   );
```

The preceding code snippet shows a diff format commonly used to represent changes made to a codebase. Here's a breakdown of the different parts:

- Lines starting with a − sign indicate code that has been removed or deleted.

- Lines starting with a + sign indicate code that has been added or inserted.

- Unchanged lines are displayed without any prefix.

In the given code snippet, the changes are represented using the diff format to clearly show what has been modified. The − lines indicate the previous code that has been removed, while the + lines indicate the new code that has been added.

After that, we can use Extract Function to map the block into a function that is in charge of rendering books by any number of given book objects.

For all public type definitions, we can create a new file types.ts and define all types in the file. Let's define a new type called Book in file types.ts, with the content:

```
type Book = {
  name: string;
}
```

And we can import and use the type like

```
import type {Book} from "./types";

const renderBooks = (books: Book[]) => {
  return <div data-test='book-list'>
    {
      books.map(book => (<div className='book-item'>
        <h2 className='title'>{book.name}</h2>
      </div>))
```

```
    }
  </div>;
}
```

Whenever the method is invoked, we can pass an array of books like so:

```
    <Typography variant='h2' component='h2' data-
    test='heading'>
    Bookish
    </Typography>
-   <div data-test='book-list'>
-     {
-       books.map(book => (<div className='book-item'>
-         <h2 className='title'>{book.name}</h2>
-       </div>))
-     }
-   </div>
+   {renderBooks(books)}
  </div>
);
```

Our tests are still passing. We improved our internal implementation without modifying the external behavior. This is a good demonstration of just one of the benefits TDD provides: easier and safer cleanup.

Refactoring – Extract Component

Now the code is much more clean and compact, but it could be better. One possible change is to modularize the code further; the granularity of abstraction should be based on component, rather than on function. For instance, we are using the function renderBooks to render a parsed array as a booklist, and we can abstract a component named BookList to do the same thing. Create a file BookList.ts and move the function renderBooks into it.

From React 16 onward, in most cases we don't need a `class` when creating a component. By using a pure function, it can be done much more easily (and with less code):

```
Import React from 'react';
import type {Book} from "./types";

const BookList = ({books}: {books: Book[]}) => {
  return <div data-test='book-list'>
    {
      books.map(book => (<div className='book-item'>
        <h2 className='title'>{book.name}</h2>
      </div>))
    }
  </div>;
}

export default BookList;
```

Now we can use this customized component just as we would any React built-in component (e.g., `div` or `h1`):

```
function App() {
  const books = [
    { name: 'Refactoring' },
    { name: 'Domain-driven design' }
  ];

  return (
    <div>
      <Typography variant='h2' component='h2' data-
      test='heading'>
      Bookish
      </Typography>
```

```
      <BookList books={books} />
    </div>
  );
}
```

With this refactoring, our code becomes more declarative and also easier to understand. Additionally, our tests remain green. You can fearlessly change the code without worrying about breaking existing functionalities. It gives you confidence to change existing code and improve the internal quality.

Talk to the Backend Server

Here's a possible revision.

Typically, the book list data should not be hard-coded in the application. In most real-life projects, this data is stored remotely on a server and needs to be fetched when the application starts up. To achieve this, we need to take the following steps:

- Configure a stub server to provide the necessary book data

- Use the axios network library to fetch the data from the server

- Use the fetched data to render our component

While we can use the native fetch API to communicate with the server, axios is a preferable option as it provides a semantic API (axios.get, axios.put, etc.) and abstractions to handle browser differences, including variations between different versions of the same browser.

Now let's examine the stub server.

Stub Server

A stub server is a commonly used tool in the development process. We'll be using a package called `json-server`. It is a node package that allows you to quickly spin up a RESTful API server with a simple JSON file as the data source. It is an easy-to-use tool that provides CRUD operations, pagination, sorting, filtering, and other features of a typical RESTful API. `Json-server` is an excellent tool for rapid prototyping, mocking, and testing of web applications.

Set Up `json-server`

Firstly, we need to install it into global space just as we did other tools:

```
npm install json-server –global
```

Then we will create an empty folder named `stub-server`:

```
mkdir -p stub-server
cd stub-server
```

After that, we create a `db.json` file with the following content:

```
{
  "books": [
    { "name": "Refactoring" },
    { "name": "Domain-driven design" }
  ]
}
```

This file defines a route and data for that route. Now we can launch the server with the following command:

```
json-server –watch db.json –port 8080
```

If you open your browser and navigate to http://localhost:8080/ books, you should be able to see something like this:

```
[
  {
    "name": "Refactoring"
  },
  {
    "name": "Domain-driven design"
  }
]
```

Of course, you can use curl to fetch it from the command line.

Make Sure the Stub Server Is Working

```
$ curl http://localhost:8080/books

[
  {
    "name": "Refactoring"
  },
  {
    "name": "Domain-driven design"
  }
]
```

Let's add a script to make life a little easier. Under scripts folder, in the package.json add in scripts section:

```
"scripts": {
  "stub-server": "json-server -watch db.json -port 8080"
},
```

We can run npm run stub-server from our root directory to get our stub server up and running. Sweet! Let's try to make some changes to the bookish application to fetch this data via HTTP calls.

Async Request in Application

Back to the application folder: bookish-react. We'll use axios for fetching data from remote service.

Installing axios in our project is easy:

```
npm install axios –save
```

Then we can use it to fetch data in our App.ts like so:

```
import React, {useEffect, useState} from 'react';
import Typography from '@mui/material/Typography';

import axios from 'axios';

import BookList from './BookList';

function App() {
  const [books, setBooks] = useState<Book[]>([]);

  useEffect(() => {
    axios.get('http://localhost:8080/books').then(res =>
    setBooks(res.data));
  }, [])

  return (
    <div>
      <Typography variant='h2' component='h2' data-
      test='heading'>
        Bookish
      </Typography>
      <BookList books={books} />
```

```
    </div>
  );
}
```

We use the React hook APIs, useState and useEffect, to manage the initial states. The useState is analogous to the this.setState API, while useEffect is used for side effects such as setTimeout or async remote calls. In the callback, we define an effect that sends an async call to localhost:8080/books, and once the data is fetched, setBooks will be called with that data, and finally BookList will be called with books from state.

You can see some output in the console from the stub server when the books API is reached when we run our application now (Figure 6-3).

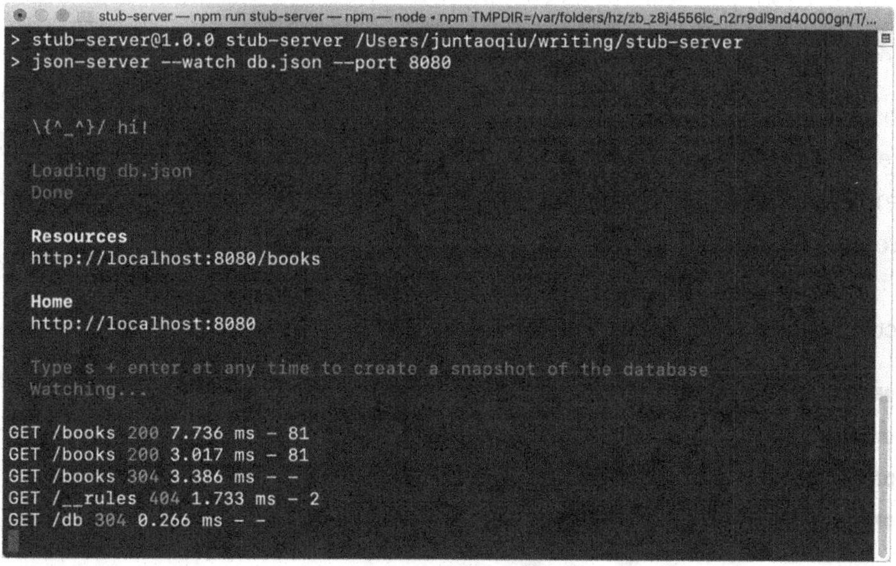

Figure 6-3. Stub server in the command line

Setup and Teardown

Let's take a closer look at our code and tests. As you can see, an implicit assumption here is that the tests *know* that the implementation will return two books. The problem with this assumption is that it makes the tests a little mysterious: Why are we expecting expect(books.length). toEqual(2), why not 3? And why are those two books Refactoring and Domain-driven design? That kind of assumption should be avoided or should be clearly explained somewhere in the tests.

One way to do this is to create some fixture data that will be set before each test and cleaned up after each test finishes.

The json-server provides a programmatic way to do it. We can define the behaviors of the stub server with some code.

Extend Stub Book Service with `middleware`

To customize json-server with custom logic (the setup and cleanups), we will need to install json-server locally. So run npm install json-server --save-dev from your command line in the stub-server folder; create a file named server.js.

And then we will need to add a middleware to accept http DELETE action with a special query string "_cleanup":

```
const jsonServer = require('json-server')
const server = jsonServer.create()
const router = jsonServer.router('db.json')
const middlewares = jsonServer.defaults()

server.use((req, res, next) => {
  if (req.method === 'DELETE' && req.query['_cleanup']) {
    const db = router.db
    db.set('books', []).write()
    res.sendStatus(204)
```

```
  } else {
    next()
  }
})

server.use(middlewares)
server.use(router)

server.listen(8080, () => {
    console.log('JSON Server is running')
})
```

This function will perform some actions based on the request method and query strings received. If the request is a DELETE request and there is a _cleanup parameter in the query string, we will clean the entity by setting the req.entity to an empty array. So when you send a DELETE to http://localhost:8080/books?_cleanup=true, this function will set the books array to empty.

With this code in place, you can launch the server with the following command:

```
node server.js
```

The complete version of the stub server code is hosted here (https://github.com/abruzzi/stub-server-for-bookish).

Once we have this middleware in place, we can use it in our test setup and teardown hooks. At the top of bookish.spec.ts, inside the describe block, add the following logic to the setup and teardown for our tests:

```
before(() => {
  return axios
    .delete('http://localhost:8080/books?_cleanup=true')
    .catch((err) => err);
});
```

```
afterEach(() => {
  return axios
    .delete('http://localhost:8080/books?_cleanup=true')
    .catch(err => err)
})

beforeEach(() => {
  const books = [
    { 'name': 'Refactoring', 'id': 1 },
    { 'name': 'Domain-driven design', 'id': 2 }
  ]

  return books.map(item =>
    axios.post('http://localhost:8080/books', item,
      { headers: { 'Content-Type': 'application/json' } }
    )
  )
})
```

Make sure to also import `axios` at the top of the file.

Before all of the tests run, we'll delete anything from the database by sending a DELETE request to this endpoint 'http://localhost:8080/books?_cleanup=true'. Then before each test is run, we insert two books into the stub server with a POST request to the URL: http://localhost:8080/books. Finally, after each test, we will clean them up.

With the stub server running, run the tests and observe what happens in the console.

beforeEach and afterEach Hook

Now we can modify the data in the setup however we want. For example, we could add another book called Building Microservices:

```
beforeEach(() => {
  const books = [
    { 'name': 'Refactoring', 'id': 1 },
    { 'name': 'Domain-driven design', 'id': 2 },
    { 'name': 'Building Microservices', 'id': 3 }
  ]

  return books.map(item =>
    axios.post('http://localhost:8080/books', item,
      { headers: { 'Content-Type': 'application/json' } }
    )
  )
})
```

And expect three books in the test:

```
it('Shows a book list', () => {
  cy.visit('http://localhost:3000/');
  cy.get('div[data-test="book-list"]').should('exist');
  cy.get('div.book-item').should((books) => {
    expect(books).to.have.length(3);

    const titles = [...books].map(x => x.querySelector('h2').
    innerHTML);
    expect(titles).to.deep.equal(
      ['Refactoring', 'Domain-driven design', 'Building
      Microservices']
    )
  })
});
```

Great! Let's take a look at what we have accomplished. Our React application is now communicating with the stub server, fetching the data, rendering it, and constructing a list. Additionally, the Cypress tests are successfully reading and writing to the stub server during the setup and teardown stages, and we've updated the end-to-end tests accordingly.

Adding a Loading Indicator

Our application is fetching data remotely, and there is no guarantee that the data will return immediately. We would like there to be some indicator of loading time to improve the user experience. Additionally, when there is no network connection at all (or a timeout), we need to show some error message.

Before we add this to the code, let's imagine how we can simulate those two scenarios:

- Slow request

- Request that failed

Unfortunately, neither of those two scenarios is easy to simulate, and even if we can, we have to couple our test with the code very tightly. Let's rethink what we want to do carefully: there are three statuses of the component (loading, error, success), so if we can test the behaviors of those three statuses in an isolated manner, then we can make sure our component is functional.

Refactor First

To make the test easy to write, we need to refactor a little first. Take a look at App.ts:

```
import type {Book} from "./types";
import BookList from "./BookList";
```

CHAPTER 6   IMPLEMENT THE BOOK LIST

```
function App() {
  const [books, setBooks] = useState<Book[]>([]);

  useEffect(() => {
    axios.get('http://localhost:8080/books').then(res =>
    setBooks(res.data));
  }, [])

  return (
    <div>
      <Typography variant='h2' component='h2' data-
      test='heading'>
        Bookish
      </Typography>
      <BookList books={books}/>
    </div>
  );
}
```

The purpose seems clear for now, but if we want to add more states the responsibility might be mixed.

Adding More States

If we want to handle cases when we have a loading or error status, we need to introduce more states to the component:

```
const App = () => {
  const [books, setBooks] = useState<Book[]>([]);
  const [loading, setLoading] = useState<boolean>(false);
  const [error, setError] = useState<boolean>(false);

  useEffect(() => {
    const fetchBooks = async () => {
      setError(false);
      setLoading(true);
```

```
    try {
      const response = await axios.get('http://
      localhost:8080/books');
      setBooks(response.data);
    } catch (e) {
      setError(true);
    } finally {
      setLoading(false);
    }
  }

  fetchBooks();
}, [])

//...
```

As it's not always necessary to show the loading and error for the entire page, we can move it into its own component, BookListContainer.ts.

Refactor: Extract Component

A simple refactoring we can do is to move the logic out of App.ts and create a new component called BookListContainer:

```
import React, {useEffect, useState} from 'react';
import axios from 'axios';
import BookList from './BookList';

const BookListContainer = () => {
  const [books, setBooks] = useState([]);
  const [loading, setLoading] = useState(false);
  const [error, setError] = useState(false);
```

```
  useEffect(() => {
    const fetchBooks = async () => {
      setError(false);
      setLoading(true);

      try {
        const res = await axios.get('http://localhost:8080/
        books');
        setBooks(res.data);
      } catch (e) {
        setError(true);
      } finally {
        setLoading(false);
      }
    };

    fetchBooks();
  }, []);

  return <BookList books={books} />
}

export default BookListContainer;
```

Then the app becomes

```
const App = () => {
  return (
    <div>
      <Typography variant='h2' component='h2' data-
      test='heading'>
        Bookish
      </Typography>
```

```
      <BookListContainer/>
    </div>
  );
}
```

That's a good start, but it has the disadvantage of coupling the network request with the rendering process, which can complicate unit tests. To simplify our testing, we'll need to separate the network request from the rendering process.

Define a React Hook

Luckily, React allows us to define our hooks in a very flexible way – using hooks. React hooks are a new addition to the React library that allows developers to use state and other React features without writing a class component. It provides a simpler and more intuitive way to manage state and lifecycle methods in functional components.

We can extract the network part out into a function called hook in useBooks.ts file:

```
const useBooks = () => {
  const [books, setBooks] = useState<Book[]>([]);
  const [loading, setLoading] = useState<boolean>(false);
  const [error, setError] = useState<boolean>(false);

  useEffect(() => {
    const fetchBooks = async () => {
      setError(false);
      setLoading(true);

      try {
        const response = await axios.get('http://
        localhost:8080/books');
        setBooks(response.data);
```

```
    } catch (e) {
      setError(true);
    } finally {
      setLoading(false);
    }
  }

  fetchBooks();
}, [])

return {
  loading,
  error,
  books
}
}
```

Here, we split all the network-related code out into a hook. In the BookListContainer, we can invoke it like this:

```
const BookListContainer = () => {
  const {loading, error, books} = useBooks();;

  // if(loading) {
  //    return <p>Loading...</p>
  // }

  // if(error) {
  //    return <p>Error...</p>
  // }

  return <BookList books={books} />
}
```

Looks pretty cool, right? The only parameter required by useBooks is the default value for BookList to render. The code is nice and clean now, and most importantly, the functional tests are still passing.

Before we jump directly into the implementation (about loading and error), let's write some unit tests for those scenarios.

Unit Tests of the Bookish Application

It's important to differentiate between end-to-end tests and unit tests. End-to-end tests simulate a user's interaction with the entire application, while unit tests isolate and test individual functions or components of the application. Although end-to-end tests are great for testing the overall functionality and flow of the application, they can be slow and cumbersome to run. Unit tests, on the other hand, are faster, more focused, and can catch bugs before they make it into the codebase.

And in this book, we'll use the React Testing Library for all the unit tests. By using the React Testing Library, we can ensure that each component is working as expected and catching errors early in the development process.

In the appendix, there is an additional chapter that covers the various types of tests and why it's important to structure them in a certain way. It provides a comprehensive overview of the testing pyramid, which distinguishes between end-to-end tests and unit tests, and explains the benefits and drawbacks of each type. By following the best practices and guidelines outlined in this chapter, you can ensure that your testing strategy is effective and efficient and that your code is reliable and maintainable.

Unit Test with the React Testing Library

The React Testing Library has already been included in create-react-app, so we can just write a few lines of code to verify the component.

Test Loading State

Now create a test file inside src called BookList.test.ts:

```
import React from 'react';
import {render, screen, within} from '@testing-library/react';

import BookList from './BookList';

describe('BookList', () => {
  it('render books', async () => {
    const props = {
      books: [
        { 'name': 'Refactoring', 'id': 1 },
        { 'name': 'Domain-driven design', 'id': 2 },
      ]
    };
    render(<BookList {...props} />);

    const headings = await screen.findAllByRole('heading')

    headings.forEach((heading, index) => {
      expect(heading).toHaveTextContent(props.
      books[index].name);
    });
  })
});
```

This is a test case that verifies the rendering of the BookList component. It creates a mock props object with an array of two book objects, and then it renders the BookList component using render() from the React Testing Library.

After that, it uses screen.findAllByRole('heading') to asynchronously find all the heading elements (which should correspond to the book titles) in the rendered component. Once all headings are found, it uses .forEach() to loop through them and verify that each heading has the expected book name by using expect(heading). toHaveTextContent(props.books[index].name).

This test case ensures that the BookList component correctly renders all the book titles provided through props.

You may be wondering if this is a duplication – haven't we already tested this case in the acceptance test? Well, *yes* and *no*. The cases in the unit tests can be used as documentation; it specifies what arguments the component requires, field names, and types. For example, in the props, we explicitly show that BookList requires an object with a books field, which is an array.

When running the tests, we will see a warning in the console:

```
console.error node_modules/react/cjs/react.development.js:172
  Warning: Each child in a list should have a unique
  'key' prop.

  Check the render method of `BookList`. See https://fb.me/
  react-warning-keys for more information.
      in div (at BookList.jsx:14)
      in BookList (at BookList.test.jsx:32)
```

This is telling us that when rendering a list, React requires a unique key for each of the items, such as id. We can quickly fix it by adding a key for each item in the loop. In our case, as each book has a unique ISBN (the International Standard Book Number), we can use it in the stub server. Now, our **final** version of BookList looks like this:

```
import React from 'react';

const BookList = ({books}) => {
  return <div data-test='book-list'>
    {
```

```
    books.map(book => (<div className='book-item'
    key={book.id}>
      <h2 className='title'>{book.name}</h2>
    </div>))
  }
  </div>;
}

export default BookList;
```

All unit tests (as shown in Figure 6-4) are passing, cool!

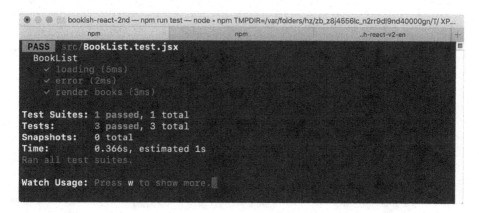

Figure 6-4. *All unit tests are passing too*

Summary

When we write tests for code, it is important to ensure that the tests are robust, reliable, and maintainable. However, sometimes the code we need to test may have a lot of external dependencies or tightly coupled dependencies that are hard to mock or test in isolation. In such cases, it can be challenging to write good tests for the code without first refactoring it.

123

Refactoring allows us to extract the dependencies out of the code, making it more modular and easier to test. By decoupling the code from its dependencies, we can create mock versions of those dependencies and test the code in isolation. This can help us to write more effective and efficient tests, as well as making the code more maintainable and extensible in the long run. So, when we encounter complicated code with lots of external dependencies, it's important to consider refactoring it first before writing tests.

And in the next chapter, we'll start to look into the implementation of the book detail page.

CHAPTER 7

Implementing the Book Detail View

In this chapter, we will focus on implementing book details using React. Our goal is to create a hyperlink for each book in the book list, allowing users to click the book's name and navigate to its dedicated detail page. This detail page will provide comprehensive information about the book, such as its title, cover image, description, reviews, and more. By developing this functionality, we aim to enhance the user experience by enabling seamless navigation and delivering specific content for each book. Let's dive into the implementation of book details and create a dynamic and engaging browsing experience for our users.

Acceptance Tests

To ensure the fulfillment of this requirement, we will begin by writing an acceptance test in our `bookish.spec.ts` file. This acceptance test will serve as a description of the desired functionality, outlining the expected behavior and verifying that the implementation meets the specified requirements. By incorporating acceptance tests into our testing suite, we can validate the functionality of the application from the user's perspective, ensuring that it aligns with the desired outcomes.

© Juntao Qiu 2023
J. Qiu, *Test-Driven Development with React and TypeScript*,
https://doi.org/10.1007/978-1-4842-9648-6_7

Let's dive into writing this acceptance test and solidify our understanding of the requirement at hand:

```
it('Goes to the detail page', () => {
  cy.visit('http://localhost:3000/');
  cy.get('div.book-item').contains('View Details').eq(0).
  click();
  cy.url().should('include', "/books/1")
});
```

Run the test, and it will fail.

Link to Detail Page

That is because we don't have a /books route yet, and we don't have the link either. To make the test pass, add a hyperlink in the BookList component:

```
    {
      books.map(book => (<div className='book-item'
      key={book.id}>
        <h2 className='title'>{book.name}</h2>
+       <a href={`/books/${book.id}`}>View Details</a>
      </div>))
    }
```

Verify Book Title on Detail Page

Then, to make sure the page shows the expected content after navigation, we need to add a line to bookish.spec.js:

```
  it('Goes to the detail page', () => {
    cy.visit('http://localhost:3000/');
```

```
    cy.get('div.book-item').contains('View Details').eq(0).
    click();
    cy.url().should('include', '/books/1');
+   cy.get('h2.book-title').contains('Refactoring');
  });
```

That checks the page has a .book-title section and its content is Refactoring. The test fails again; let's fix it by adding client-side routing to our application.

As you can see, there is a page navigation here: the user will be able to jump to the detail page when clicking a button. That means we need some mechanism to maintain the router.

Frontend Routing

We need to add react-router and react-router-dom as dependencies. react-router and react-router-dom are essential libraries for managing routing in React applications.

react-router is the core library that provides the routing functionality, allowing you to define routes and navigate between different views or components in your application. It provides a flexible and declarative approach to handling routing, enabling you to create dynamic and seamless user experiences.

react-router-dom is a companion library that builds upon react-router by providing specific routing components designed for web applications. It includes components like BrowserRouter and Link that are tailored for browser-based routing.

Together, react-router and react-router-dom offer a powerful and intuitive routing solution for React applications. They enable you to handle complex routing scenarios, including nested routes, route parameters, and query parameters. With these libraries, you can create single-page applications (SPAs) with multiple views and seamless navigation between them.

Whether you're building a simple portfolio website or a sophisticated web application, react-router and react-router-dom are indispensable tools for managing navigation and creating a smooth user experience. By incorporating these libraries into your React projects, you can easily handle routing and ensure that your application responds to user interactions in a seamless and intuitive manner:

```
npm install react-router react-router-dom --save
```

In index.tsx, we import BrowserRouter and wrap it around <App />. This means the whole application can share the global Router configurations:

```
import { BrowserRouter as Router } from "react-router-dom";
import App from "./App";

const root = ReactDOM.createRoot(
  document.getElementById("root") as HTMLElement
);

root.render(
  <Router>
    <App />
  </Router>
);
```

We then define two routes in App.tsx:

```
import Typography from "@mui/material/Typography";
import BookListContainer from "./BookListContainer";
import BookDetailContainer from "./BookDetailContainer";

import { Routes, Route } from "react-router-dom";

function App() {
  return (
```

```
<div>
  <Typography variant="h2" component="h2" data-test="heading">
    Bookish
  </Typography>
  <Routes>
    <Route path="/" element={<BookListContainer />} />
    <Route path="/books/:id"
    element={<BookDetailContainer />} />
  </Routes>
</div>
);
}
```

With those routes, when the user accesses root path /, the component BookListContainer will be rendered. When /books/123 is visited, BookDetailContainer will be displayed.

BookDetailContainer Component

Finally, we need to create a new file BookDetailContainer.tsx. It will be pretty similar to the first version of BookListContainer.tsx, except that the id of the book will be extracted by a hook useParams from react-router. Once we have the book id, we can send an HTTP request to fetch the book details from the server side:

```
import React, { useEffect, useState } from "react";
import axios from "axios";

import { useParams } from "react-router";
import { Book } from "./types";

const BookDetailContainer = () => {
  const { id } = useParams<string>();
  const [book, setBook] = useState<Book>();
```

```
useEffect(() => {
  const fetchBook = async () => {
    const book = await axios.get(`http://localhost:8080/
    books/${id}`);
    setBook(book.data);
  };

  fetchBook();
}, [id]);

return (
  <div className="detail">
    <h2 className="book-title">{book && book.name}</h2>
  </div>
);
};

export default BookDetailContainer;
```

Great, the functional tests are now passing, as shown in Figure 7-1.

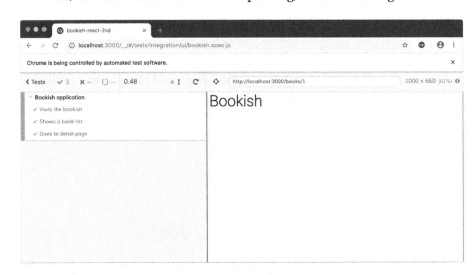

Figure 7-1. *Redirect to the detail page*

Extract useBook Hook

However, the data fetching process could be improved. It's time for us to refactor the useBook to fit the new requirement. Because we have higher-level tests ready, we can confidently make some changes:

```
export const useBook = () => {
  const { id } = useParams<string>();
  const [book, setBook] = useState<Book>({ id: 0, name: "" });
  const [loading, setLoading] = useState<boolean>(false);
  const [error, setError] = useState<boolean>(false);

  useEffect(() => {
    const fetchBook = async () => {
      try {
        const book = await axios.get(`http://localhost:8080/
        books/${id}`);
        setBook(book.data);
      } catch (e) {
        setError(true);
      } finally {
        setLoading(false);
      }
    };

    fetchBook();
  }, [id]);

  return {
    book,
    loading,
    error,
  };
};
```

We defined a new hook called useBook to manage the data fetching and state management. And in the calling place, we can simply put

```
const {book, loading, error} = useBook();
```

Simplify BookDetailContainer with the New Hook

And for BookDetailContainer, it then can be simplified as

```
import React from "react";
import { useBook } from "./useBook";

const BookDetailContainer = () => {
  const { book } = useBook();

  return (
    <div className="detail">
      <h2 className="book-title">{book && book.name}</h2>
    </div>
  );
};

export default BookDetailContainer;
```

The code now looks much cleaner.

Unit Tests

In the end-to-end test, we just make sure there is a title in the detail page. If we add more details to the page, such as description, and book cover, we check for them in the lower-level test – the unit test. Unit tests run fast and check more for specific details than end-to-end tests, making it easier for developers to debug if something goes wrong.

Refactoring

Extract Presentational Component BookDetail

Even though in BookDetailContainer there is only a single line to render the details, it's a good idea to extract that line out to a separate component – we'll call it BookDetail:

```
const BookDetail = ({ book }: { book: Book }) => {
  return (
    <div className="detail">
      <h2 className="book-title">{book.name}</h2>
    </div>
  );
};

export default BookDetail;
```

BookDetailContainer can then be simplified as

```
const BookDetailContainer = () => {
  const { book } = useBook();

  return <BookDetail book={book} />;
};
```

Let's check all the tests now: the Cypress tests are all passing, but your unit tests may be red with the following error message:

```
console.error
  Error: Uncaught [Error: useRoutes() may be used only in
  the context of a <Router> component.]
```

The error message is stating that the useRoutes hook from React Router is being used outside the context of a <Router> component.

The useRoutes hook is part of the React Router library, which is used to manage and create navigation in React applications. Hooks like useRoutes must be used within components that are children of a <Router> component. This is because they rely on the context provided by the <Router> to function correctly.

And also if you are using react-router version 6 or higher, you will get the following errors:

● BookList › render books

Invariant failed: You should not use <Link> outside a <Router>

The <Link> component is used to create links in your application, and it must be used within a <Router> component because it uses the router's context to function.

In addition, you will see something wrong with axios with jest at the moment:

Jest encountered an unexpected token

    SyntaxError: Cannot use import statement outside a module

    1 | import {useEffect, useState} from "react";
    2 | import {Book} from "./types";
  > 3 | import axios from "axios";

Let's fix the axios issue very quickly and then look into the react-router in test. You will need to modify the package.json and add a new section for jest:

```
"jest": {
  "moduleNameMapper": {
    "axios": "axios/dist/node/axios.cjs"
  }
},
```

Now let's look into the router problem.

MemoryRouter for Testing

To fix that, we need to modify BookList.test.ts a little by providing a <MemoryRouter>. In React Router, the MemoryRouter is a specialized router component that allows you to manage routing within the memory of your application, rather than relying on the browser's URL history.

The MemoryRouter provides a router implementation that stores the current location and history in memory, making it useful for scenarios where you don't need to update the browser's URL or navigate between pages in a traditional sense.

This component is particularly handy for testing or scenarios where you want to manage routing programmatically without affecting the browser's URL. It allows you to simulate navigation and track location changes within the memory of your application.

With MemoryRouter, you can define routes, render components based on those routes, and programmatically manipulate the current location and history stack. This provides greater control and flexibility for scenarios where you need to manage routing within the context of your application's memory.

Whether you're writing tests, creating custom navigation logic, or handling nontraditional routing scenarios, the MemoryRouter component in React Router offers a valuable tool for managing routing within the memory of your application.

We add a wrapper inside the render. This will wrap whatever component you passed in inside a MemoryRouter. Then we can invoke the renderWithRouter instead of render in all the tests that need to render a Link.

In the React Testing Library, using a custom render function is a common practice that offers several benefits. By leveraging custom render functions, you can enhance code organization, reduce duplication, and promote consistency in your testing approach.

To use a custom render function properly, follow these steps:

1. Create a helper function, such as `renderWithRouter`, that wraps the `render` function from the React Testing Library.

2. In the helper function, apply any default configurations or set up logic you want to use consistently across tests.

3. Return the result of calling the original `render` function with the provided component and any additional options.

4. Export the custom render function for use in your test files.

Let's define our custom render function `renderWithRouter`:

```
import { MemoryRouter as Router } from "react-router-dom";

const renderWithRouter = (component: JSX.Element) => {
  return {
    ...render(<Router>{component}</Router>),
  };
};
```

In your test files, you can then import and use the `renderWithRouter` function instead of the default `render` function from the React Testing Library. This allows you to benefit from the additional setup or configuration provided by your custom render function.

```
it("render books", async () => {
  const props = {
    books: [
      { name: "Refactoring", id: 1 },
      { name: "Domain-driven design", id: 2 },
```

```
    ],
  };

  renderWithRouter(<BookList {...props} />);

  const headings = await screen.findAllByRole("heading");

  headings.forEach((heading, index) => {
    expect(heading).toHaveTextContent(props.books[index].name);
  });
});
```

Book Detail Page

Book Title

Now we can quickly add unit tests in file BookDetail.test.ts in order to drive the implementation:

```
describe("BookDetail", () => {
  it("renders title", () => {
    const props = {
      book: {
        id: 1,
        name: "Refactoring",
      },
    };

    render(<BookDetail {...props} />);

    const title = screen.getByRole("heading");
    expect(title.innerHTML).toEqual(props.book.name);
  });
});
```

This test will pass because we already render the name field.

Book Description

Let's add some more fields. We'll start from a unit test this time and use that to drive out the implementation:

```
it("renders description", () => {
  const props = {
    book: {
      id: 1,
      name: "Refactoring",
      description:
        "Martin Fowler's Refactoring defined core ideas and
        techniques " +
        "that hundreds of thousands of developers have used to
        improve " +
        "their software.",
    },
  };

  render(<BookDetail {...props} />);

  const description = screen.getByText(props.book.description);
  expect(description).toBeInTheDocument();
});
```

But as we've changed the interface of Book type, we will need to update the type definition first:

```
export type Book = {
  id: number;
  name: string;
  description?: string;
}
```

A straightforward implementation could look like this:

```
const BookDetail = ({ book }: { book: Book }) => {
  return (
    <div className="detail">
      <h2 className="book-title">{book.name}</h2>
      <p className="book-description">{book.description}</p>
    </div>
  );
};
```

With all tests now successfully passing, the codebase is adorned with a delightful shade of green. However, it's time to take a step back and consider ways to improve the overall structure of the project. One observation that has caught my attention is the burgeoning size of the project structure as more files were created. It seems to be expanding beyond desirable boundaries, warranting a closer examination and potential restructuring to enhance organization and maintainability. Let's explore strategies to address this issue and ensure a more streamlined and manageable codebase.

File Structure

Our current file structure lacks hierarchy, with all the files residing in a single folder. This flat structure is considered a code smell and can lead to difficulties in locating specific files. To address this issue, let's embark on a restructuring endeavor that promotes better organization and ease of navigation.

Currently, our files look like this:

```
src
├── App.tsx
├── BookDetail.tsx
├── BookDetail.test.tsx
├── BookDetailContainer.tsx
├── BookList.tsx
├── BookList.test.tsx
├── BookListContainer.tsx
├── hooks.ts
├── types.ts
└── index.tsx
```

There are multiple ways to split an application into modules and organize them. I have found splitting the application by feature makes the most sense to me after having tried all of the different combinations across various projects.

Modularize

So for now, let's define two separate folders: BookDetail and BookList for feature one and feature two, respectively.

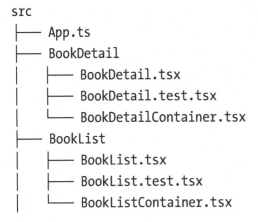

```
src
├── App.ts
├── BookDetail
│   ├── BookDetail.tsx
│   ├── BookDetail.test.tsx
│   └── BookDetailContainer.tsx
├── BookList
│   ├── BookList.tsx
│   ├── BookList.test.tsx
│   └── BookListContainer.tsx
```

```
├── hooks.ts
├── types.ts
└── index.tsx
```

This organized folder structure significantly improves the ability to locate specific components that need to be modified. It enhances readability and makes it easier for developers to navigate through the project, fostering a more efficient and seamless development experience.

Testing Data

You may find it a little tricky to clean up all the data for functional tests. And when you want to check how the application looks in the browser manually, there is no data at all.

Let's fix this problem by introducing another `database` file for `json-server`:

```
{
  "books": [
    {
      "name": "Refactoring",
      "id": 1,
      "description": "Martin Fowler's Refactoring defined core
      ideas and techniques ..."
    },
    {
      "name": "Domain-driven design",
      "id": 2,
      "description": "Explains how to incorporate effective
      domain modeling into the software development process."
    },
    {
```

```
    "name": "Building Microservices",
    "id": 3,
    "description": "Author Sam Newman provides you with a
    firm grounding in the concepts while ..."
  },
  {
    "name": "Acceptance Test Driven Development with React",
    "id": 4,
    "description": "This book describes how to apply the
    Acceptance Test Driven Development ..."
  }
 ]
}
```

and save the content as books.json in the stub-server folder. Now update the stub-server script in package.json:

```
json-server --watch books.json --port 8080
```

And run the server: npm run stub-server (Figure 7-2).

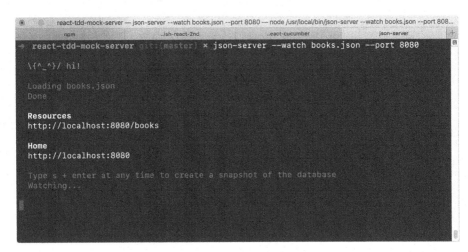

Figure 7-2. *Start stub server*

Remember to run the end-to-end tests here as well. As we're changing the data expected in the book list, we'll also need to change what the tests expect. As the server is doing the job of mocking out all the data, you'll notice we don't need the beforeEach and afterEach at this point.

User Interface Refinement

After successfully completing two thrilling and demanding features, it's time to turn our attention to the user interface (as you can tell in Figure 7-3, it doesn't look really impressive), which is currently lacking visual appeal. To address this, we will embark on a journey to enhance the styling and aesthetics of our application.

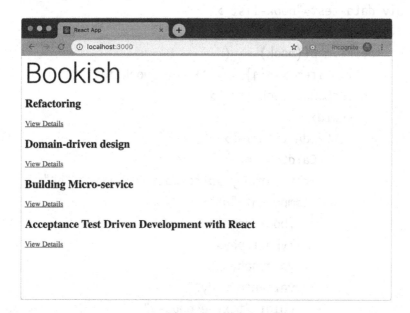

Figure 7-3. *The UI is not appealing*

Within the realm of Material UI, an extensive collection of UI components awaits, offering both fundamental and advanced functionalities. Among these offerings is a remarkable addition called the responsive grid system. This grid system provides valuable assistance in creating flexible and adaptable layouts for your application. With Material UI's arsenal at our disposal, we gain access to a wide range of UI components and convenient tools, empowering us to design intricate and visually appealing user interfaces.

Using Grid System

In our case, let's implement the Grid and Card components to our BookList:

```
const BookList = ({ books }: { books: Book[] }) => {
  return (
    <div data-test="book-list">
      <Grid container spacing={3}>
        {books.map((book) => (
          <Grid item xs={4} sm={4} key={book.id}
          className="book-item">
            <Card>
              <CardActionArea>
                <CardContent>
                  <Typography gutterBottom variant="h5"
                  component="h2">
                    {book.name}
                  </Typography>
                  <Typography
                    variant="body2"
                    color="textSecondary"
                    component="p"
                  >
                    {book.description}
                  </Typography>
```

```
              </CardContent>
            </CardActionArea>
            <CardActions>
              <Button size="small" color="primary">
                <Link to={`/books/${book.id}`}>View
                Details</Link>
              </Button>
            </CardActions>
          </Card>
        </Grid>
      ))}
    </Grid>
  </div>
  );
};
```

There are a few things going on here:

1. The Grid component from Material UI is used to create the grid layout. It has a container property to specify that it acts as the container for the grid items. The spacing property defines the space between the grid items.

2. Within the Grid component, the books array is mapped using the map function. For each book in the array, a Grid item is rendered.

3. Each Grid item has a fixed size based on the xs (extra small) and sm (small) screen breakpoints. In this case, each item spans four columns on extra small and small screens.

4. Inside each `Grid` item, a `Card` component from
    Material UI is used to display book information. It
    consists of a `CardActionArea`, `CardContent`, and
    `CardActions`.

5. The book's name and description are displayed
    using `Typography` components from Material UI.

6. The `CardActions` component contains a `Button`
    component with a link to view more details
    about the book. The link is wrapped inside a `Link`
    component from React Router and is generated
    dynamically based on the book's `id`.

Handling Default Value

We have a new requirement to address: the backend service's data may
occasionally include unexpected null values in certain fields. To ensure
a seamless user experience, we must handle these cases gracefully. For
instance, the `description` field might not always be present and could
contain an empty string or null value.

In such situations, we should gracefully handle this scenario by using
the book's name as a fallback for the description. By implementing this
fallback mechanism, we can ensure consistent and informative content
presentation, even when unexpected null values arise in the backend data.

A Failing Test with `undefined`

We can add a test to describe this case, noting the props object doesn't
contain a `description` field at all:

```
it("displays the book name when no description was
given", () => {
  const props = {
    book: {
      id: 1,
      name: "Refactoring",
    },
  };

  render(<BookDetail {...props} />);

  const description = screen.getByTestId("book-description");
  expect(description).toHaveTextContent(props.book.name);
});
```

Then our test failed again, as you can see in Figure 7-4.

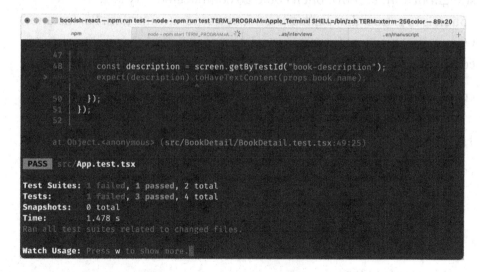

Figure 7-4. Book description cannot be found

We can fix that with a conditional operator:

```
const BookDetail = ({ book }: { book: Book }) => {
  return (
    <div className="detail">
      <h2 className="book-title">{book.name}</h2>
      <p className="book-description" data-testid="book-
      description">
        {book.description ? book.description : book.name}
      </p>
    </div>
  );
};
```

It's worth noting the `conditional` operator here. It's pretty
straightforward for now. But it could go complicated very fast. A better
option is to extract that expression out as a separate function. For instance,
we can use an extract function to isolate that potential change into a pure
computing function:

```
const getDescriptionFor = (book: Book) => {
  return book.description ? book.description : book.name;
};

const BookDetail = ({ book }: { book: Book }) => {
  return (
    <div className="detail">
      <h2 className="book-title">{book.name}</h2>
      <p className="book-description" data-testid="book-
      description">
        {getDescriptionFor(book)}
```

```
    </p>
  </div>
  );
};
```

In this particular case, there is no requirement to extract a function. However, it is important to be cautious and mindful of scenarios like this. When performing calculations within the rendering process, it is advisable to exercise extra caution as it requires more attention. The goal is to keep the rendering logic as simple and straightforward as possible. By being vigilant and mindful of such cases, we can maintain a clean and efficient rendering process, contributing to the overall performance and maintainability of our code.

One Last Change?

Now let's consider another change: if the length of description is greater than 300 characters, we need to truncate the content at 300 characters and show a Show more... link. When a user clicks the link, the full content will be displayed.

We can add a new test for this case:

```
it('Shows *more* link when description is too long', () => {
  const props = {
    book: {
      id: 1,
      name: 'Refactoring',
      description: 'The book about how to do refactoring ....'
    }
  };

  render(<BookDetail {...props} />);
```

```
  const link = screen.getByText('Show more...');
  expect(link).toBeInTheDocument();

  const description = screen.getByTestId("book-description");
  expect(description).toHaveTextContent('The book about how to
  do refactoring ....');
})
```

This compels us to write or modify the code to fulfill the requirement. After ensuring that all tests pass successfully, we can proceed with refactoring. This entails extracting methods, creating new files, reorganizing methods or classes, renaming variables, adjusting folder structures, and more.

Refactoring is an ongoing and iterative process. It provides us with endless opportunities to enhance the codebase. Whenever time allows, we can repeat this process multiple times, continuously improving the code until we achieve a clean and self-documenting state.

By dedicating effort to refactoring, we can optimize code readability, maintainability, and overall quality. Through consistent iterations, we strive to create code that is not only functional but also clear, expressive, and easy to understand.

Summary

In this chapter, we embarked on the journey of implementing the book detail section, ensuring a seamless user experience. We began by writing a Cypress test to verify the functionality at a high level. This test served as our guiding requirement throughout the implementation process.

Next, we utilized the power of the React Testing Library to define additional edge cases, validating the behavior at a lower level. By thoroughly testing different scenarios, we ensured robust functionality and caught any potential issues.

To enhance the visual appeal of the user interface, we incorporated Material UI, leveraging its rich library of components and styling capabilities. This allowed us to create an appealing and cohesive design for displaying book details.

Furthermore, we recognized the importance of maintaining an organized and navigable project structure. To address this, we undertook the restructuring of the folder hierarchy, promoting ease of navigation and improving code discoverability. This reorganization facilitated efficient collaboration and enhanced the overall maintainability of the project.

Throughout this chapter, we focused on delivering a polished and comprehensive book detail section, aligning with user expectations and providing an enhanced reading experience. By combining Cypress tests, the React Testing Library, Material UI, and improved folder structure, we created a visually pleasing book detail section. Let's move forward with confidence, knowing that our implementation is both functional and visually appealing.

CHAPTER 8

Searching by Keyword

Welcome to the third feature of our journey, where we dive into the implementation of search functionality by book name. This feature plays a crucial role in enhancing user experience, particularly when dealing with extensive book lists. As the list grows beyond a single screen or page, it becomes increasingly challenging for users to locate specific books. Therefore, enabling users to effortlessly search for books by name becomes an invaluable addition to our application.

In this chapter, we will focus on implementing the search feature, empowering users to quickly find desired books by simply entering their names. By incorporating this functionality, we aim to streamline the book discovery process and provide users with a seamless and efficient browsing experience.

With the search feature in place, users will no longer need to scroll through lengthy book lists, trying to spot the books they are seeking. Instead, they can easily input the book's name and have the relevant results instantly displayed, saving time and improving overall satisfaction.

Acceptance Test

As previously, we start by writing an `acceptance test`:

```
it('Searches for a title', () => {
  cy.visit('http://localhost:3000/');
  cy.get('div.book-item').should('have.length', 4);
```

© Juntao Qiu 2023
J. Qiu, *Test-Driven Development with React and TypeScript*,
https://doi.org/10.1007/978-1-4842-9648-6_8

```
cy.get('[data-test="search"] input').type('design');
cy.get('div.book-item').should('have.length', 1);
cy.get('div.book-item').eq(0).contains('Domain-driven
design');
});
```

In this test scenario, we simulate the action of entering the keyword "design" into the search input box and verify that the book list only displays the book titled "Domain-driven design." By executing this test, we aim to ensure that the search functionality accurately filters the book list based on the provided keyword, displaying only the relevant results. Let's proceed with this test, validating the expected behavior of the search feature and ensuring its effectiveness in delivering precise search results to the user.

The simplest way to implement this feature is to modify the `BookListContainer` by adding a `TextField` from `Material UI` to it:

```
return (<>
  <TextField
    label='Search'
    value={term}
    data-test='search'
    onChange={(e) => setTerm(e.target.value)}
    margin='normal'
    variant='outlined'
  />
  <BookList books={data} loading={loading} error={error}/>
</>);
```

We'll need to introduce `state` to the component – before the return statement, add the following line, remembering to import `useState` from react:

```
const [term, setTerm] = useState('');
```

154

When the term (the search term) changes, we want to trigger a new search. We can make use of the useEffect hook, something like

```
useEffect(() => {
  performSearch(`http://localhost:8080/books?q=${term}`)
}, [term]);
```

Wait a minute, this logic looks familiar. We have similar logic in useBooks already, right? It would be much easier for us to modify the useBooks to make it more generic to support search as well.

The useBooks is defined as follows:

```
const useBooks = () => {
  const [books, setBooks] = useState<Book[]>([]);
  const [loading, setLoading] = useState<boolean>(false);
  const [error, setError] = useState<boolean>(false);

  useEffect(() => {
    const fetchBooks = async () => {
      setError(false);
      setLoading(true);

      try {
        const response = await axios.get(
          "http://localhost:8080/books?_sort=id"
        );
        setBooks(response.data);
      } catch (e) {
        setError(true);
      } finally {
        setLoading(false);
      }
    };
```

```
    fetchBooks();
  }, []);

  return {
    loading,
    error,
    books,
  };
};
```

So we need to introduce the `term` or `keyword` state into the hook and expose the `setter` so that whenever a user typed something, we can trigger a refetch:

```
const [term, setTerm] = useState<string>('');

useEffect(() => {
  const fetchBooks = async (term: string) => {
    setError(false);
    setLoading(true);

    try {
      const response = await axios.get(`http://localhost:8080/
      books?q=${term}&_sort=id`);
      setBooks(response.data);
    } catch (e) {
      setError(true);
    } finally {
      setLoading(false);
    }
  }

  fetchBooks(term);
}, [term])
```

Note that we are using books?q=${e.target.value} as the URL to fetch data. There is a full-text searching API provided by json-server; you can send books?q=domain to the backend, and it will return all the content that contains the domain.

You can verify the API on the command line like this:

```
curl http://localhost:8080/books?q=domain
```

So the only change in BookListContainer is that we use the term and setTerm from the useBooks hook:

```
const BookListContainer = () => {
  const { books, term, setTerm } = useBooks();

  return <>
    <TextField
      label='Search'
      value={term}
      data-test='search'
      onChange={(e) => setTerm(e.target.value)}
      margin='normal'
      variant='outlined'
    />
    <BookList books={books} />
  </>;
};
```

Now our tests are green again (as shown in Figure 8-1). Let's jump to the next step of the Red-Green-Refactor cycle.

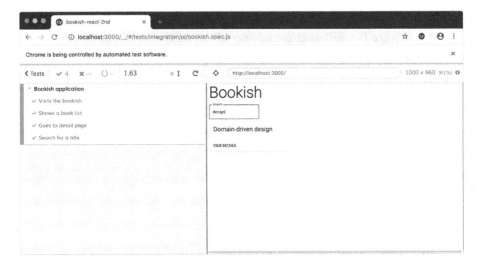

Figure 8-1. *Search by book title*

One Step Further

Let's say someone else wants to use the search box we just finished on this page, how can we reuse it? It's tough because currently the search box is very tightly coupled with the rest of the code in BookListContainer, but we can extract it into another component, called SearchBox:

```
import { TextField } from "@mui/material";

const SearchBox = ({
  term,
  onSearch,
}: {
  term: string;
  onSearch: (term: string) => void;
}) => {
  return (
```

```
  <TextField
    label="Search"
    value={term}
    data-test="search"
    onChange={(e) => onSearch(e.target.value)}
    margin="normal"
    variant="outlined"
  />
 );
};

export default SearchBox;
```

After that extraction, BookListContainer becomes

```
const BookListContainer = () => {
  const { books, term, setTerm } = useBooks();

  return (
    <>
      <SearchBox term={term} onSearch={setTerm} />
      <BookList books={books} />
    </>
  );
};
```

Now let's add a unit test:

```
describe("SearchBox", () => {
  it("renders input", () => {
    const props = {
      term: "",
      onSearch: jest.fn(),
    };
```

```
    render(<SearchBox {...props} />);
    const input = screen.getByRole("textbox");
    userEvent.type(input, "domain");

    expect(props.onSearch).toHaveBeenCalled();
  });
});
```

We are using jest.fn() to create a spy object that can record the trace of invocations. We use a userEvent.type API to simulate a change event with domain as it's the payload. We can then expect that the onChange method has been called.

Let's add one more requirement here: when performing a search, we don't want white-space to be part of the request. So we trim the string before it's sent to service. Let's write a test first:

```
it('trim empty strings', () => {
  const props = {
    term: '',
    onSearch: jest.fn()
  }

  render(<SearchBox {...props} />);
  const input = screen.getByRole("textbox");
  userEvent.type(input, ' ');

  expect(props.onSearch).not.toHaveBeenCalled();
})
```

It will fail because we currently send any and all values to the books API. To fix it, we can define a function in SearchBox that will intercept the event before it reaches the upper level:

```
const performSearch = (event: any) => {
  const value = event.target.value;
```

```
if(value && value.trim().length === 0) {
    return;
}

onSearch(value);
}
```

and use the function as onChange instead of calling onSearch directly:

```
return (
    <TextField
        label="Search"
        value={term}
        data-test="search"
        onChange={performSearch}
        margin="normal"
        variant="outlined"
    />
);
```

The successful results are shown in Figure 8-2.

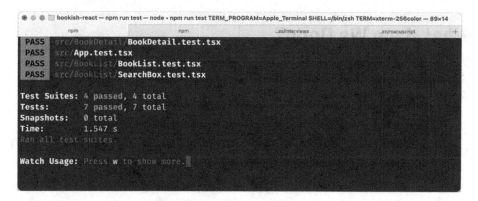

Figure 8-2. *Searching is working as expected*

Throughout our development process, we adopted a comprehensive testing approach that encompassed both end-to-end and lower-level tests. We initiated the testing phase with an end-to-end test, focusing on the successful execution of the happy path scenario. This test allowed us to ensure that our application's key functionality was functioning as intended, providing a seamless user experience.

From the foundation, we carefully constructed lower-level tests that covered various scenarios and edge cases to confirm our components worked as intended, even under difficult conditions. These tests increased our coverage depth and helped us spot and fix unexpected issues. By mixing end-to-end and lower-level tests, we created a thorough testing environment that handled both typical and unusual scenarios, ensuring our application's performance and enhancing its resilience against unexpected challenges.

Our testing efforts served as a valuable tool for quality assurance, facilitating the identification of potential weaknesses and areas for improvement. With a thorough testing suite in place, we can confidently deploy our application, knowing that it has undergone rigorous evaluation and can deliver a reliable and satisfying user experience.

What Have We Done?

Fantastic! We have successfully completed all three features, and it's time for a quick review of our accomplishments:

- We have developed three pure components, namely, BookDetail, BookList, and SearchBox, along with their corresponding unit tests. These components form the foundation of our application, providing essential functionality and ensuring code quality through thorough testing.

- Additionally, we have implemented two container components, BookDetailContainer and BookListContainer. These container components bridge the gap between the pure components and the data layer, facilitating data management and state manipulation.

- To handle data fetching efficiently, we have created a custom hook dedicated to this purpose. This hook streamlines the process of retrieving data, promoting code reusability and maintainability.

- To ensure the overall functionality of our application, we have devised four acceptance tests. These tests cover the most valuable paths, including list viewing, detailed book information, and searching. By encompassing these critical areas, we have provided comprehensive test coverage, assuring the reliability and accuracy of our application.

By accomplishing these milestones, we have laid a solid foundation for our application's success. We can confidently proceed, knowing that we have created a set of robust components, incorporated effective data fetching mechanisms, and validated our features through rigorous testing. Let's celebrate our achievements and move forward with pride as we continue to build upon this strong framework.

Moving Forward – The Test Code Is As Important

Maybe you have already noticed some code smells in our end-to-end tests. We're utilizing many fancy commands without expressing exactly what we are doing in terms of business value:

```
it("Shows a book list", () => {
  cy.visit("http://localhost:3000/");
  cy.get('div[data-test="book-list"]').should("exist");

  cy.get("div.book-item").should((books) => {
    expect(books).to.have.length(4);
    const titles = [...books].map((x) => x.querySelector("h2").
    innerHTML);

    expect(titles).to.eql([
      "Refactoring",
      "Domain-driven design",
      "Building Microservices",
      "Acceptance Test Driven Development with React",
    ]);
  });
});
```

By introducing a few functions, we can improve the readability significantly:

```
const gotoApp = () => {
  cy.visit('http://localhost:3000/');
}

const checkAppTitle = () => {
  cy.get('h2[data-test="heading"]').contains('Bookish');
}
```

And in the test cases, we can make use of them like this:

```
it('Visits the bookish', () => {
  gotoApp();
  checkAppTitle();
});
```

For complicated functions, we can abstract even more:

```
const checkBookListWith = (expectation = []) => {
  cy.get('div[data-test="book-list"]').should('exist');
  cy.get('div.book-item').should((books) => {
    expect(books).to.have.length(expectation.length);

    const titles = [...books].map(x => x.querySelector('h2').
    innerHTML);
    expect(titles).to.deep.equal(expectation)
  })
}
```

And use it like this:

```
checkBookListWith([
  "Refactoring",
  "Domain-driven design",
  "Building Microservices",
  "Acceptance Test Driven Development with React",
]);
```

or

```
const checkSearchedResult = () => {
  checkBookListWith(['Domain-driven design'])
}
```

After we have extracted a few functions, some patterns emerge. We can do some further refactoring:

```
describe('Bookish application', () => {
  beforeEach(() => {
    feedStubBooks();
    gotoApp();
  });
```

```
afterEach(() => {
  cleanUpStubBooks();
});

it('Visits the bookish', () => {
  checkAppTitle();
});

it('Shows a book list', () => {
  checkBookListWith(['Refactoring', 'Domain-driven design',
  'Building Microservices']);
});

it('Goes to the detail page', () => {
  gotoNthBookInTheList(0);
  checkBookDetail();
});

it('Search for a title', () => {
  checkBookListWith(['Refactoring',
    'Domain-driven design',
    'Building Microservices',
    'Acceptance Test Driven Development with React']);
  performSearch('design');
  checkBookListWith(['Domain-driven design']);
});
});
```

The result is not only visually appealing but also demonstrates a significant separation between the business value and implementation details. This separation holds potential benefits for future endeavors, such as the possibility of migrating to another testing framework or rewriting specific components.

With a clear distinction between these aspects, it becomes evident to any reader or developer, making future modifications and adaptations more straightforward. This deliberate approach of separating concerns not only contributes to the overall cleanliness of the codebase but also ensures its long-term maintainability and adaptability.

Summary

In the preceding three chapters, we embarked on an immersive journey of developing three essential features for our application, Bookish. Along the way, we gained valuable insights into the practical implementation of Acceptance Test–Driven Development (ATDD) in a real-world project.

We began by swiftly setting up the React environment, ensuring a seamless development experience. Utilizing the mock server, we successfully launched a mock service, enabling us to simulate various scenarios for testing purposes.

With the aid of Cypress, we meticulously crafted acceptance tests, forming the backbone of our testing strategy. By adhering to the classic Red-Green-Refactor cycle, we adopted an iterative approach, ensuring that our code passed the defined acceptance tests and refining it through continuous refactoring. During the refactoring phase, we focused on code smells, applying responsible code splitting, method extraction, class renaming, and folder restructuring to improve code readability and maintainability.

Furthermore, we explored extensions for json-server, enhancing our testing capabilities by facilitating data preparation and cleanup before and after test execution. This streamlined the test scenarios, making them more readable, self-contained, and independent.

Finally, we discovered the power of refactoring Cypress commands into meaningful functions, enhancing the overall readability and comprehension of our test suite.

Through this chapter, we have not only acquired practical knowledge of ATDD but also honed our skills in creating clean, maintainable code. With our newfound understanding, we are equipped to tackle future development challenges while upholding best practices in testing and code organization.

CHAPTER 9

Introduction to State Management

Welcome to the chapter on state management with Redux using `@reduxjs/toolkit`. Here, we'll explore how Redux can simplify and streamline your React application's state management. Throughout this chapter, we'll cover essential Redux concepts such as actions, reducers, and the Redux store. We'll focus on leveraging the features provided by `@reduxjs/toolkit` to write clean and concise code.

You'll learn how to define actions and reducers using the `createSlice` function, which greatly simplifies the process. Additionally, we'll dive into handling asynchronous operations using `createAsyncThunk`, ensuring smooth integration with APIs and data fetching.

Testing Redux slices is also a crucial part of the chapter. We'll explore how to write comprehensive tests using popular frameworks like Jest, guaranteeing the reliability of your state management logic.

By the end of this chapter, you'll have a solid understanding of state management with Redux using `@reduxjs/toolkit`. You'll be able to efficiently handle complex state changes in your React applications, resulting in more organized and maintainable code. Get ready to unlock the power of Redux and elevate your state management game!

© Juntao Qiu 2023
J. Qiu, *Test-Driven Development with React and TypeScript*,
https://doi.org/10.1007/978-1-4842-9648-6_9

State Management

Over time, frontend development has grappled with the intricate task of synchronizing state across various components. Managing state in scenarios like search boxes, tab statuses, and routing has proven to be perplexing and demanding, despite the introduction of MVVM (Model View View-Model) libraries like Backbone or the two-way data binding offered by Angular. In the earlier days, the concept of "components" as we know them today was absent, and only DOM (Document Object Model) fragments existed within the jQuery realm.

However, in today's web development landscape, we encounter a whole new realm with increasingly complex interactions and data transformations. Consequently, the approach to handling these complexities has undergone significant transformations.

A Typical Scenario of Building UI

Let's take a look at the page shown in Figure 9-1 as an example.

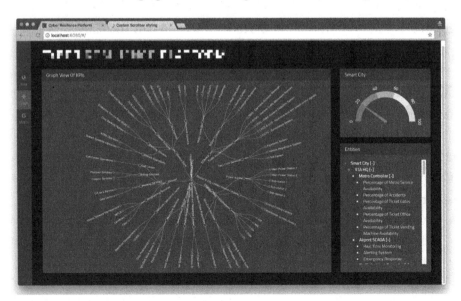

Figure 9-1. *A network monitoring application*

There is a graph component in the middle of the page and a tree component on the right-hand side. When a node on the tree is clicked, it should collapse or expand based on its previous status, and the status change should be synchronized with the graph.

If you don't use an external library, using customized DOM events may cause a `dead-loop` – when you have to register a listener on `graph` to listen to changes to the `tree`, also do the same thing to the tree. And when an event is triggered, it will bounce back and forth between those two components. And when you have more than just two components, things will soon go south.

A more reliable method is to extract the underlying data and use the Pub-Sub pattern: the tree and graph are all listening to changes in the data; once the data changes, components should re-render themselves.

Pub-Sub Pattern

The Publish-Subscribe (Pub-Sub) pattern is a messaging pattern commonly used in software architectures to facilitate communication between different components or modules. It provides a means for decoupling the sender (publisher) and receiver (subscriber) of messages, enabling them to interact without direct knowledge of each other.

In the Pub-Sub pattern, entities known as publishers generate messages or events. These are dispatched to a centralized hub, and the hub operates as a mediator, delivering these messages to all corresponding subscribers that have indicated interest in these types of messages.

Subscribers, on the other hand, express their interest in specific types of messages by subscribing to relevant topics or channels within the pub-sub system. When a publisher sends a message to the pub-sub system, it is then broadcasted to all subscribers who have expressed interest in that particular topic.

The key advantage of the Pub-Sub pattern is its decoupling nature. Publishers and subscribers can operate independently, without direct dependencies on each other. This loose coupling enables better scalability, as new publishers or subscribers can be added or removed dynamically without affecting the overall system.

Additionally, the Pub-Sub pattern promotes flexibility and extensibility. Publishers and subscribers can evolve independently, making it easier to introduce new functionality or modify existing components without disrupting the entire system.

By leveraging the Pub-Sub pattern, software architectures can achieve loose coupling, scalability, and flexibility, enabling efficient communication between components and enhancing the overall resilience and maintainability of the system.

Implementations of this pattern in frontend pages are prevalent nowadays. You can find it on almost every web page. You can implement your own pub-sub library. However, you will likely find it tedious and hard to maintain. Fortunately, we have other options.

When the underlying data is changed, either by a user event on the browser, a timer, or an async service call, we need an easy way to manage those changes and make sure the data model is always reflected to the latest data across all the components.

A Brief of Redux

Redux is a predictable state container for JavaScript applications. It provides a way to manage and update the state of your application in a predictable and centralized manner. It is often used in large-scale applications where state management can become complex, but can be used in any application where you want to have more control over how state is managed.

The main principle of using Redux is the separation of concerns between the UI components and the application state. UI components should only be concerned with rendering data, and not with managing it.

All state changes should be handled by Redux, and UI components should be updated based on the changes in the state. This separation allows for a more modular and reusable codebase and makes it easier to reason about the state of the application.

Redux achieves this by having a single store that holds the state of the entire application. This store can only be updated by dispatching actions, which are objects that describe the changes to be made to the state. These actions are handled by reducers, which are pure functions that take the current state and an action as input and return a new state based on the action. The updated state is then propagated to all the components that depend on it, triggering a re-render of the UI.

It provides a simple and effective way to test and debug your application, as well as track its state. Although it's not specific to any particular library or framework, it's most commonly used in conjunction with React.

Three Principles of Redux

In Redux, there are three principles that form its foundation:

- All state is stored in a single global data source.

- State is immutable or read-only.

- Changes are made using pure functions.

Whenever a change occurs, such as a user clicking a button or receiving data from a backend, an action is created in the form of a JavaScript object that describes the change. This action then goes through a reducer function, which specifies how the application state will change in response to the action. The reducer function takes in the previous state and the action and returns the new state. By following these principles, testing and debugging become straightforward, as the state can be easily tracked and traced.

173

Although Redux is not bound to any specific library or framework, it is most used with React.

React and Redux work well together because React provides an efficient way to render the view and Redux provides a simple and predictable way to manage the application state. By using them together, developers can build complex applications with ease and keep the codebase organized and maintainable.

Decoupling Data and View

If you take a close look at our useBooks hook, you will notice that it's actually doing a number of things:

```
const useBooks = () => {
  const [books, setBooks] = useState<Book[]>([]);
  const [loading, setLoading] = useState<boolean>(false);
  const [error, setError] = useState<boolean>(false);

  const [term, setTerm] = useState<string>('');

  useEffect(() => {
    const fetchBooks = async (term: string) => {
      setError(false);
      setLoading(true);

      try {
        const response = await axios.get
        (`http://localhost:8080/books?q=${term}&_sort=id`);
        setBooks(response.data);
      } catch (e) {
        setError(true);
      } finally {
        setLoading(false);
      }
    }
```

```
    fetchBooks(term);
  }, [term])

  return {
    loading,
    error,
    books,
    term,
    setTerm
  }
}
```

In the hook code

1. It makes a request for data to an external service.

2. It takes care of URL changes.

3. It manages several statuses, including `loading` and `error`.

Some of those statuses will always be updated together, for example:

```
{
  books: [],
  loading: false,
  error: false
}
```

or

```
{
  error: true
}
```

These states undergo changes due to various factors. For instance, network requests alter the loading and error states, user interactions on the page determine the value of the "term" state, and the "books" state is populated through asynchronous function calls.

By utilizing Redux, we can establish a global store that accurately reflects the application state. Additionally, we employ reducers to handle state modifications originating from different sources. When an action is triggered within the UI, resulting in state modifications, the updated data is propagated to the relevant components for re-rendering.

This is where the state management container plays a crucial role. The container takes charge of essential tasks such as monitoring changes, dispatching actions, reducing state, and broadcasting changes. By abstracting these details, the container simplifies the overall state management process, ensuring smooth synchronization and seamless interaction between components.

The Formula: view = f(state)

The formula `view = f(state)` represents the relationship between the state and the view in a software application. It signifies that the view, or the user interface, is determined by the current state of the application. As the state changes, the view is updated accordingly to reflect the new state.

In this formula, `f` represents the function or logic that transforms the state into the appropriate view representation. This function takes the current state as input and produces the corresponding view output.

By adhering to this formula, developers can ensure that the user interface accurately reflects the underlying state of the application. As the state evolves, the view is dynamically updated, providing users with a responsive and interactive experience.

The `view = f(state)` formula is a fundamental concept in reactive and declarative programming paradigms, allowing for efficient and maintainable UI development. It promotes a clear separation between state management and view rendering, facilitating easier debugging, testing, and future enhancements to the application.

```
const state = {
  books: [
    {
      'name': 'Refactoring',
      'id': 1,
      'description': 'Refactoring'
    },
    {
      'name': 'Domain-driven design',
      'id': 2,
      'description': 'Domain-driven design'
    },
    {
      'name': 'Building Microservices',
      'id': 3,
      'description': 'Building Microservices'
    }
  ],
  term: ''
}
```

When the user types `Domain` in the search box, the state snapshot becomes

```
const state = {
  books: [
    {
```

```
      'name': 'Domain-driven design',
      'id': 2,
      'description': 'Domain-driven design'
    }
  ],
  term: 'Domain'
}
```

These two pieces of data (state) can represent the whole application at a point. Since view = f(state), for any given state, the view is always predictable, so the only thing the application developer cares about is how to manipulate the data, as the UI will render automatically.

Implementing State Management
Environment Setup

Firstly, we need to add some packages to enable us to use redux:

```
npm install @reduxjs/toolkit react-redux --save
```

Historically, Redux requires very verbose and repetitive code. And then the Redux team decided to wrap a few most common libraries together and call it @reduxjs/toolkit.

@reduxjs/toolkit simplifies Redux development by providing utilities, such as configureStore for easy store configuration and sensible defaults. It introduces "slices" for concise reducer and action creation. It handles immutable updates using immer and includes built-in support for Redux DevTools Extension. Additional utilities like createAsyncThunk, createSelector, and createEntityAdapter enhance functionality.

We can start with the state design.

Firstly, we can define a new type:

```
type AppStateType = {
  books: Book[];
  loading: boolean;
  error: boolean;
  term: string;
};
```

This type will be our application state, and initially we might have the following data for initializing our application:

```
const initialState: AppStateType = {
  books: [],
  loading: false,
  error: false,
  term: "",
};
```

There aren't any books in the page, both loading and error are defined as false, and also there isn't a keyword set. And at some point, we'll need to trigger an event to fetch data from the backend – and at the moment, that is done by the useBooks hook.

Define a Slice

With @reduxjs/toolkit, we can define a slice. A slice is a portion of the Redux state that corresponds to a specific feature or domain within your application. It encapsulates the state, actions, and reducers related to that particular feature.

Create a file bookListSlice.ts as follows:

```
export const bookListSlice = createSlice({
  name: "books",
  initialState: initialState,
  reducers: {
    setTerm: (state, action) => {
      state.term = action.payload;
    },
  }
});

export const { setTerm } = bookListSlice.actions;

export default bookListSlice.reducer;
```

The code snippet defines a Redux slice for managing a list of books. The slice is named "books" and has an initial state defined as initialState.

Within the reducers object, there is a single action called "setTerm." This action is associated with a reducer function that takes the current state and the action payload as parameters. When the "setTerm" action is dispatched (being called in the UI, for example), it updates the term property of the state to the value provided in the action payload.

The bookListSlice.actions object contains the action creators for the defined actions. In this case, it includes the setTerm action creator. And the bookListSlice.reducer represents the reducer function for the slice.

By exporting the setTerm action creator and the reducer function, other parts of the application can import and use them to dispatch actions and handle state updates related to the "books" slice.

Fetching Data from Remote

There will be some changes needed in the container component.
So instead of using the useBooks hook for the book list, we will
need to define an async action in Redux. This can be done with the
createAsyncThunk API:

```
export const fetchBooks = createAsyncThunk<Book[], string>(
  "books/search",
  async (term: string = "") => {
    const response = await axios.get(
      `http://localhost:8080/books?q=${term}&_sort=id`
    );
    return response.data;
  }
);
```

The function fetchBooks is using the createAsyncThunk function
provided by Redux Toolkit:

- It takes two generic type parameters: Book[] specifies
  the type of the action payload, and string specifies the
  type of the term parameter.

- The first argument to createAsyncThunk is the **type** of
  the action, which is set to "books/search".

- The second argument is an async function that handles
  the asynchronous logic. It receives the term parameter
  and makes an HTTP GET request to fetch books
  from the server using the provided term as a query
  parameter.

- The response data is then returned as the fulfilled value
  of the action.

181

There will be three possible results from this action: a fulfilled promise with a book list, a rejected state when something went wrong, and a pending state indicating the ongoing process.

We'll need to expand the bookListSlice with a new section called extraReducers:

```
export const bookListSlice = createSlice({
  //...
  extraReducers: (builder) => {
    builder.addCase(fetchBooks.fulfilled, (state, action) => {
      state.books = action.payload;
      state.loading = false;
    });

    builder.addCase(fetchBooks.pending, (state) => {
      state.loading = true;
    });

    builder.addCase(fetchBooks.rejected, (state) => {
      state.error = true;
      state.loading = false;
    });
  },
});
```

And for the preceding code snippet

- The extraReducers field allows you to define additional reducer logic that responds to specific action types.

- Within the extraReducers, builder is used to add case reducers for different action types.

- The addCase function is called for each action type, followed by the corresponding case reducer function.

- In this example, `fetchBooks.fulfilled` is an action type that represents a successful completion of the `fetchBooks` async action.

- The case reducer for `fetchBooks.fulfilled` updates the `state` by assigning the `action.payload` (the fetched books) to the `books` property and sets `loading` to `false`.

- Similarly, there are case reducers defined for `fetchBooks.pending` and `fetchBooks.rejected` actions, which update the `state` accordingly based on the pending and rejected states of the `fetchBooks` async action.

By including these extra reducers, Redux will automatically handle the asynchronous action defined in `fetchBooks`. The state updates for different stages of the async action (such as pending, fulfilled, or rejected) will be taken care of by Redux. This allows us to conveniently access and utilize this state within our application.

Define the Store

In a store, you can combine many slices together to configure the global state (in file `store.ts`):

```
import { configureStore } from '@reduxjs/toolkit'
import bookListReducer from './bookListSlice';

const store = configureStore({
  reducer: {
    list: bookListReducer
  }
});

export default store;
```

183

The code snippet demonstrates the configuration and setup of a Redux store using @reduxjs/toolkit. Let's break down the code:

1. The configureStore function is imported from @reduxjs/toolkit. It is used to create and configure the Redux store.

2. The bookListReducer (imported from './bookListSlice') is passed as the reducer for the "app" key in the reducer object.

3. The configureStore function is called with the reducer configuration to create the Redux store.

By configuring the store in this way, the Redux store is set up with a single reducer (bookListReducer) under the "app" key.

And also we'll need to export the types for React components to reference, allowing for type-safe usage of the Redux store and actions throughout the application:

```
export type RootState = ReturnType<typeof store.getState>
export type AppDispatch = typeof store.dispatch;
```

Once we have the store configured, we can then use the store in the application root. That means apart from the **Router** we introduced in the previous chapter, we'll wrap the whole application with **Provider** from react-redux. And the only required prop for the provider is the store, so that all the children nodes can access the store with hooks:

```
import { Provider } from "react-redux";
import store from "./store";

const root = ReactDOM.createRoot(
  document.getElementById('root') as HTMLElement
);
```

```
root.render(
  <Provider store={store}>
    <Router>
      <App/>
    </Router>
  </Provider>
);
```

Fantastic, now we have all the necessary parts ready. Our application is still functioning at the moment, the hooks are used, and there is an empty store defined. The tests are all passing as well.

Migrate the Application

Before integrating Redux into our container component, we need to make some modifications to the tests. This is necessary because the hooks used in the component rely on accessing a provider to access the state:

```
import { Provider } from "react-redux";
import store from "./store";

const customRender = (component: JSX.Element) => {
  return {
    ...render(
      <Provider store={store}>
        <Router>
          {component}
        </Router>
      </Provider>
    )
  }
}
```

And the App.test.tsx will be updated to

```
it('renders bookish', () => {
  customRender(<App />);
  const heading = screen.getByText(/Bookish/i);
  expect(heading).toBeInTheDocument();
});
```

Book List Container

```
import { useDispatch, useSelector } from "react-redux";
import { fetchBooks } from "../bookListSlice";

import type { AppDispatch, RootState } from "../store";

const BookListContainer = () => {
  const { term, setTerm } = useBooks();
  const { books } = useSelector((state: RootState) => ({
    books: state.list.books,
  }));

  const dispatch = useDispatch<AppDispatch>();

  useEffect(() => {
    dispatch(fetchBooks(""));
  }, [dispatch]);

  return (
    <>
      <SearchBox term={term} onSearch={setTerm} />
      <BookList books={books} />
    </>
  );
};

export default BookListContainer;
```

The updated code snippet shows the `BookListContainer` component that utilizes Redux with React:

- The `useSelector` hook is used to select the `books` state from the Redux store. The selected state is assigned to the `books` variable.

- The `useDispatch` hook is used to get the dispatch function, typed with the `AppDispatch` type.

- An effect is used with the `useEffect` hook to dispatch the `fetchBooks` action with an empty string as the term. This will trigger the async action to fetch books when the component mounts.

Note here the `useSelector` hook from "react-redux" allows React components to select and retrieve specific data from the Redux store. It automatically subscribes to changes in the selected data and triggers re-rendering when the data changes.

The preceding code mixes the `useBooks` hook and `useSelector`, which should be avoided as we have moved the logic from hook to Redux.

Refine the SearchBox

The change to the SearchBox component is a bit different. We need to trigger the `setTerm` action from SearchBox, so it's kind of making the SearchBox know the existence of the outside world.

And we should consider modifying the tests first. Let's define a mockStore so we can `dispatch` action to and verify the `state` against:

```
import { configureStore } from "@reduxjs/toolkit";
import bookListReducer from "../bookListSlice";
```

```
const mockStore = configureStore({
  reducer: {
    list: bookListReducer,
  },
});
```

And then in each test, we'll wrap our SearchBox component around a provider with the mockStore passed in:

```
it("renders input", () => {
  const mockStore = configureStore({
    reducer: {
      list: bookListReducer,
    },
  });

  render(
    <Provider store={mockStore}>
      <SearchBox />
    </Provider>
  );
  const input = screen.getByRole("textbox");

  act(() => {
    userEvent.type(input, "domain");
  });

  const state = mockStore.getState();
  expect(state.list.term).toEqual("domain");
});
```

Now let's make sure the SearchBox is using our new Redux to trigger reducers:

```
const SearchBox = () => {
  const dispatch = useDispatch<AppDispatch>();
```

```
const performSearch = (event: any) => {
  const value = event.target.value;
  if (value && value.trim().length === 0) {
    return;
  }

  dispatch(setTerm(value));
  dispatch(fetchBooks(value));
};

return (
  <TextField
    label="Search"
    data-test="search"
    onChange={performSearch}
    margin="normal"
    variant="outlined"
  />
);
};
```

Note here when the keyword is not empty, we'll dispatch two actions: setTerm and fetchBooks. The fetchBooks is an async action, and as mentioned earlier, Redux will handle all this and manipulate loading and error correspondingly.

Test Individual Reducers

You may have observed that the previous tests resemble **integration tests** as they interact with various components of the application, including state management, UI components, and reducers. However, there are scenarios where you may prefer to focus on lower-level tests, specifically unit tests.

In these cases, the emphasis is on testing the logic within reducers without considering the UI aspect:

```
import bookListReducer, { setTerm } from "./bookListSlice";
describe("bookListReducer", () => {
  const initialState = {
    term: "",
    books: [],
    loading: false,
    error: false,
  };

  it("should handle setTerm action", () => {
    const action = setTerm("Refactoring");
    const newState = bookListReducer(initialState, action);

    expect(newState.term).toEqual("Refactoring");
  });
});
```

This test case ensures that the bookListReducer handles the setTerm action correctly by updating the term property in the state with the provided payload.

Book Details Slice

Similarly to the book list slice, we can define a separate slice for book details:

```
export const fetchBookDetails = createAsyncThunk<Book, string>(
  "bookDetails/fetch",
  async (id) => {
```

```
  const response = await axios.get(`http://localhost:8080/
  books/${id}`);
  return response.data;
 }
);
```

Also, we need to define the slice data type, as well as the slice itself:

```
type BookDetailType = {
  book: Book;
  loading: boolean;
  error: boolean;
};

const initialState: BookDetailType = {
  book: {
    id: 0,
    name: "",
  },
  loading: false,
  error: false,
};

const bookDetailsSlice = createSlice({
  name: "bookDetails",
  initialState: initialState,
  reducers: {},
  extraReducers: (builder) => {
    builder
      .addCase(fetchBookDetails.pending, (state) => {
        state.loading = true;
        state.error = false;
      })
```

```
    .addCase(fetchBookDetails.fulfilled, (state, action) => {
      state.book = action.payload;
      state.loading = false;
    })
    .addCase(fetchBookDetails.rejected, (state, action) => {
      state.loading = false;
      state.error = true;
    });
  },
});
```

Once we have the reducers defined and exported, in the store.ts we can merge these two reducers together:

```
import { configureStore } from '@reduxjs/toolkit'
import bookListReducer from './bookListSlice';
import bookDetailsReducer from './bookDetailSlice';

const store = configureStore({
  reducer: {
    list: bookListReducer,
    detail: bookDetailsReducer
  }
});
```

And the corresponding BookDetailsContainer component will be modified into something like

```
const BookDetailContainer = () => {
  const { id = "" } = useParams<string>();
  const { book } = useSelector((state: RootState) => ({
    book: state.detail.book,
  }));
```

```
const dispatch = useDispatch<AppDispatch>();

useEffect(() => {
  dispatch(fetchBookDetails(id));
}, [dispatch]);

  return <BookDetail book={book} />;
};

export default BookDetailContainer;
```

Do You Need a State Management Library?

When considering whether you need a state management library for your application, it's essential to evaluate the complexity of your state management requirements. State management libraries like Redux can be beneficial for large-scale applications with complex state interactions, where maintaining data consistency and managing state across multiple components becomes challenging.

If your application involves a shared state that needs to be accessed and modified by multiple components, or if you find yourself passing props through multiple levels of component hierarchy, a state management library can help simplify your code and improve maintainability.

State management libraries shine when handling scenarios such as caching data, managing global application state, handling asynchronous actions, or implementing undo/redo functionality. These libraries offer tools and patterns for organizing, updating, and accessing state in a predictable and centralized manner.

On the other hand, for smaller applications with simpler state needs, introducing a state management library may add unnecessary complexity. React's built-in state management capabilities, like component state and context API, might be sufficient to handle the state requirements.

For applications like Bookish, as we have demonstrated thus far, a state management library may not be necessary. Utilizing hooks and, at most, the context API can provide sufficient state management capabilities. However, it is crucial to understand the advantages and considerations of using a state management library when the need arises, as well as how to effectively test the relevant components in an application.

Many legacy systems currently employ Redux as their state management solution, and it offers valuable protection against errors through comprehensive test coverage. While Redux can be a powerful tool, it is important to assess whether its implementation is warranted based on the specific requirements and complexity of your project. By weighing the benefits and trade-offs, you can make an informed decision about when and where to leverage a state management library like Redux.

Summary

Throughout this chapter, we successfully integrated Redux into our application, replacing the useBooks custom hook with Redux state management. This transition allowed us to centralize and manage our application's state more efficiently.

We refactored the SearchBox and BookListContainer components to utilize Redux by dispatching actions and accessing state through the useSelector and useDispatch hooks. This restructuring improved the overall organization and maintainability of our codebase.

In addition, we ensured the reliability of our Redux implementation by writing comprehensive tests. By covering a wide range of scenarios, we confirmed that our actions, reducers, and state management logic functioned correctly. All tests passed successfully, giving us confidence in the stability of our application.

By adopting Redux, we achieved a more structured and scalable approach to state management. Separating concerns between components and state management logic led to cleaner code and improved maintainability. With Redux, we can confidently handle complex state changes and provide a better user experience in our React application.

In conclusion, we successfully integrated Redux into our project, refactored components to utilize Redux state management, and validated our implementation with comprehensive tests. With a robust Redux foundation in place, our application is now equipped to handle complex state requirements and adapt to future growth and enhancements.

CHAPTER 10

Book Reviews

Welcome to the chapter on implementing review functionality in our application. In this chapter, we will explore how to enable users to create and update reviews for books. Reviews provide valuable insights and feedback, allowing users to share their opinions and experiences with others.

To achieve this, we will make changes to both the backend and frontend components. We will modify the backend using json-server to support the creation and update of reviews as subresources of books. This will involve defining routes and handling requests accordingly.

On the frontend, we will integrate the review functionality into our Redux store by adding a new slice. This slice will contain the necessary actions and reducers to manage review-related state, such as creating, updating, and retrieving reviews.

Throughout the chapter, we will focus on writing tests to ensure the correctness and reliability of our review implementation. We will cover various testing techniques, including unit tests for actions and reducers, as well as integration tests to verify the interaction between components.

By the end of this chapter, you will have a solid understanding of how to implement review functionality, test your code effectively, and enable users to provide valuable feedback on books within your application. Let's dive in and get started!

In any real-world project, you usually have to deal with some type of resource management. An advertising management system manages a schedule or a campaign by creating, modifying, or deleting items under

© Juntao Qiu 2023
J. Qiu, *Test-Driven Development with React and TypeScript*,
https://doi.org/10.1007/978-1-4842-9648-6_10

some business restriction. An HR system would help HR to manage employee records by creating (when the company has new hires), modifying (being promoted), and deleting (retiring). If you look at the problem those systems are trying to solve, you will find a similar pattern: they're all applying CRUD (Create, Read, Update, Delete) operations on some resources.

However, not all systems have to involve all four operations; for a critical system, no data will be deleted – the programmer will just set a flag in the record to mark them as deleted. The records are still there, but the user cannot retrieve them from the GUI anymore.

In this chapter, we'll learn how to implement a classic set of CRUD operations on the review resource by extending our application bookish, with ATDD applied of course.

Business Requirements

The book detail page showcases important details such as the book's title, description, and cover image. However, to enrich the user experience and provide deeper insights, we want to integrate user reviews. Reviews offer valuable perspectives from readers, expressing their opinions about the book. These reviews can vary from positive to negative, often accompanied by ratings, enabling users to assess the overall reception and quality of the book.

Let's start with the simplest scenario when there are no reviews. We need to render an empty container – we'll call it reviews-container.

Start with an Empty List

```
describe("ReviewList", () => {
  it("renders an empty list", () => {
    const reviews = [
```

```
      {
        id: 1,
        bookId: 1,
        name: "Juntao Qiu",
        date: "2023/06/01",
        content: "Excellent work, really impressed by your
        efforts",
      },
    ];

    render(<ReviewList reviews={reviews} />);
    expect(screen.getByTestId("reviews-container")).
    toBeInTheDocument();
  });
});
```

It should be simple to make the test pass:

```
type Review = {
  id: number;
  bookId: number;
  name: string;
  date: string;
  content: string;
}

const ReviewList = ({reviews}: {reviews: Review[]}) => {
  return <div data-testid="reviews-container" />
}

export default ReviewList;
```

Rendering a Static List

Our second test case can involve some static data:

```
it("renders a list when data is passed", () => {
  const reviews = [
    {
      id: 1,
      bookId: 1,
      name: "Juntao Qiu",
      date: "2023/06/21",
      content: "Excellent work, really impressed by your
      efforts",
    },
    {
      id: 2,
      bookId: 1,
      name: "Abruzzi Kim",
      date: "2023/06/22",
      content: "What a great book",
    },
  ];

  render(<ReviewList reviews={reviews} />);

  const items = screen.getAllByTestId("review");

  expect(items.length).toBe(2);
});
```

Here, we are demonstrating how to use the component from the outside (pass in an array of reviews, each of which has fields for name, date, and content). It would be possible for other programmers to reuse our component without looking into our implementation.

A simple map should work for us. Since the map requires a unique identity for the key attribute, let's combine the name and date to form a key; in the following section, we will create an id when we integrate with the backend API.

```
const ReviewList = ({ reviews }: { reviews: Review[] }) => {
  return (
    <div data-testid="reviews-container">
      {reviews.map((review) => (
        <div data-testid="review" key={review.id}>{review.
        content}</div>
      ))}
    </div>
  );
};
```

Use the Review Component in BookDetail

To kick off our first integration, we'll begin by implementing the test for the integration between ReviewList and BookDetail. As you may have already gathered, our approach follows the test-first methodology.

We can add a new test case in BookDetail.test.tsx as we want to verify if the BookDetail has a ReviewList on it:

```
it("renders reviews", () => {
  const props = {
    book: {
      id: 1,
      name: "Refactoring",
      description:
        "Martin Fowler's Refactoring defined core ideas and
        techniques...",
      reviews: [
```

```
      {
        id: 1,
        bookId: 1,
        name: "Juntao",
        date: "2023/06/21",
        content: "Excellent work, really impressed by your
        efforts",
      },
    ],
  },
};

render(<BookDetail {...props} />);

const reviews = screen.getAllByTestId("review");
expect(reviews.length).toBe(1);
expect(reviews[0].innerHTML).toEqual(
  "Excellent work, really impressed by your efforts"
);
});
```

In the implementation phase, we introduce the ReviewList component, which takes the reviews attribute as a prop. With the power of componentization, this integration becomes straightforward and requires minimal additional code:

```
const BookDetail = ({ book }: { book: Book }) => {
  return (
    <div className="detail">
      <h2 className="book-title">{book.name}</h2>
      <p className="book-description" data-testid="book-
      description">
        {getDescriptionFor(book)}
      </p>
```

```
      {book.reviews && <ReviewList reviews={book.reviews} />}
    </div>
  );
};
```

Fulfill a Book Review Form

We can generate some static data to display in the BookDetail component, but it would be better if we can show some real data from the end user. We need a simple form for the user to communicate their point of view about the book. For now, we can provide two input boxes and a submit button. The first input is for the user's name (or email address), and the second (a textarea) is used for the review content.

We can add a new test case in the BookDetail component:

```
it("renders review form", () => {
  const props = {
    book: {
      id: 1,
      name: "Refactoring",
      description:
        "Martin Fowler's Refactoring defined core ideas and
        techniques...",
    },
  };

  render(<BookDetail {...props} />);

  const nameInput = screen.getByTestId("name");
  const contentInput = screen.getByTestId("content");
  const button = screen.getByTestId("submit");
```

```
expect(nameInput).toBeInTheDocument();
expect(contentInput).toBeInTheDocument();
expect(button).toBeInTheDocument();
});
```

Make sure the <form> is displayed under the description section and above reviews. The TextField and Button components can both be imported from Material UI:

```
import { Button, TextField } from "@mui/material";
```

Now we have to connect it to state:

```
const BookDetail = ({ book }: { book: Book }) => {
  const [name, setName] = useState<string>("");
  const [content, setContent] = useState<string>("");

  const dispatch = useDispatch<AppDispatch>();

  return (
    <div className="detail">
      <h2 className="book-title">{book.name}</h2>
      <p className="book-description" data-testid="book-
      description">
        {getDescriptionFor(book)}
      </p>

      <form noValidate autoComplete="off">
        <TextField
          value={name}
          onChange={(e) => setName(e.target.value)}
        />

        <TextField
          data-testid="content"
```

```
      value={content}
      onChange={(e) => setContent(e.target.value)}
    />

    <Button
      data-testid="submit"
    >
      Submit
    </Button>
  </form>

  {book.reviews && <ReviewList reviews={book.reviews} />}
  </div>
  );
};
```

To ensure data persistence, we need to make corresponding changes in the backend service. This may involve modifying the API endpoints or adding new endpoints specifically for handling review data. By aligning the frontend and backend, we can establish a seamless connection and ensure the successful storage and retrieval of review data.

End-to-End Test

As you may have observed, our approach in this function began with the unit test of the ReviewList component. This choice was influenced by the static nature of the changes, as there were no behavioral interactions involved at this stage. In such cases, you can opt to start either from the top with an end-to-end test or from the bottom with the individual component. Personally, I find it beneficial to begin with the component itself as it allows for more rapid feedback, facilitating the implementation process.

The end-to-end test can be summarized as follows: navigate to the detail page, locate the input fields, enter relevant content, and click the submit button. Upon completion, we anticipate that the submitted content will be displayed on the page.

```
it('Write a review for a book', () => {
  gotoNthBookInTheList(0);
  checkBookDetail('Refactoring');

  cy.get('input[name="name"]').type('Juntao Qiu');
  cy.get('textarea[name="content"]').type('Excellent work!');
  cy.get('button[name="submit"]').click();

  cy.get('div[data-test="reviews-container"] .review').
    should('have.length', 1);
});
```

The test will fail after the click, as it neither sends the data to the server nor receives a response and re-renders (Figure 10-1).

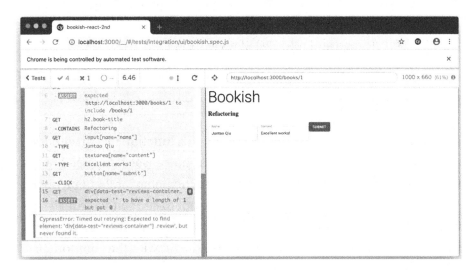

Figure 10-1. *The cypress test is now failing*

To make the test pass, we'll need to send a post request to the backend and then refresh the page to get the latest data for that particular book. We can start by adding a new redux slice.

Define a Review Slice

We have learned that all network activity and other chores are handled by actions in redux. So let's first define an action to create a `review`:

```
type AddReviewRequest = {
  id: number;
  name: string;
  content: string;
};
export const addReview = createAsyncThunk<Review,
AddReviewRequest>(
  "reviews/addReview",
  async ({ id, name, content }: AddReviewRequest) => {
    try {
      const response = await axios.post(
        `http://localhost:8080/books/${id}/reviews`,
        {
          name,
          content,
        }
      );
      return response.data;
    } catch (error) {
      throw error;
    }
  }
);
```

In this code snippet, we have the definition of an async thunk addReview using createAsyncThunk from Redux Toolkit. It takes an AddReviewRequest object as its first parameter, representing the required data to add a review.

The AddReviewRequest type specifies the shape of the object, including properties such as id (book ID), name (reviewer's name), and content (review content).

Within the addReview async thunk, an axios.post request is made to the specified URL endpoint (http://localhost:8080/books/${id}/reviews) with the provided name and content data. If the request is successful, the response data is returned.

The async thunk is created with a specific type annotation using <Review, AddReviewRequest>. This signifies that the fulfilled action of addReview will return a value of type Review, representing the newly added review object.

In case of any errors during the API call, an error handling block is included to catch and handle any potential exceptions. The throw error statement rethrows the error to propagate it further if necessary.

By utilizing createAsyncThunk and defining the addReview async thunk, you can easily handle the asynchronous operation of adding a review and manage the associated state updates within your Redux application.

We're assuming that when we POST some data to the endpoint http://localhost:8080/books/1/reviews, a new review will be created for the book with id 1:

```
{
  "name": "Juntao Qiu",
  "content": "Excellent work!"
}
```

Then we add an onClick event handler in the form in the BookDetail component:

```
<Button
  variant='contained'
  color='primary'
  name='submit'
  onClick={() => dispatch(addReview({ id: book.id, name,
  content }))}
>
  Submit
</Button>
```

The unit tests for BookDetail are now failing because useDispatch can only be used within a Provider. We can fix that by

```
import { Provider } from "react-redux";
import store from "../redux/store";

const renderWithProvider = (component: JSX.Element) => {
  return {
    ...render(<Provider store={store}>{component}</Provider>),
  };
};
```

and use renderWithProvider wherever render is being used:

```
renderWithProvider(<BookDetail {...props} />);
```

Adjust the Stub Server for Book Reviews

We have been utilizing json-server as a convenient tool for our backend API needs. To align with our new requirement, we need to customize it further. Specifically, we want to establish a relationship between review and book by treating `review` as a subresource of a book. This enables us to access all the reviews associated with a specific book by making a request to /books/1/reviews.

Furthermore, we aim to include all the `reviews` as embedded resources within the /books/1 response. This simplifies the rendering process of the book detail page. To achieve this, we must define a corresponding `route` in `json-server` with the following configuration:

```
server.post('/books/:id/reviews', (req, res) => {
  const { id } = req.params;
  const { name, content } = req.body;

  const book = router.db.get('books').find({ id:
  parseInt(id) }).value();
  if (book) {
    if(!book.reviews) {
      book.reviews = [];
    }

    const review = { id: book.reviews.length+1, bookId:
    parseInt(id), name, content };

    book.reviews.push(review);
    router.db.write();

    res.status(201).json(review);
  } else {
    res.status(404).json({ error: 'Book not found' });
  }
});
```

The preceding code snippet is a custom route handler for the POST `/books/:id/reviews` endpoint in `json-server`. It performs the following steps:

1. Extracts the `id`, `name`, and `content` from the request parameters and body

2. Retrieves the corresponding book based on the `id` from the `books` collection in the JSON file

3. If the book exists, generates a new ID for the review and creates a review object with the provided details

4. Checks if the book has a `reviews` array and initializes it if it doesn't

5. Adds the new review to the book's `reviews` array

6. Writes the updated data back to the JSON file

7. Sends a response with the newly created review if successful or an error message if the book is not found

Note that to encode the json object from the request body, we'll need a middleware `body-parser`. So in the stub server folder, we can install the `body-parser` package first and then make the following changes in `server.js`:

```
const bodyParser = require('body-parser');

server.use(bodyParser.json());
server.use(bodyParser.urlencoded({ extended: true }));
```

Whenever you access `/books/1`, it returns all the reviews along with the response. For example, if we send a request like this through curl in the command line:

```
curl http://localhost:8080/books/1
```

we would get the response like

```
{
  "name": "Refactoring",
  "id": 1,
  "description": "Martin Fowler's Refactoring defined core
  ideas...",
  "reviews": [
    {
      "id": 1,
      "bookId": 1,
      "name": "Juntao",
      "content": "Great book!"
    }
  ]
}
```

Great work! Also, when we send POST request with a review data to http://localhost:8080/books/1/reviews, it will create a review under the book with id 1. Now, we can create the review via the form shown in Figure 10-2.

Figure 10-2. *The stub server is supporting add reviews*

Of course, we will need to refresh the page after the submission to see the newly created review:

```
const dispatch = useDispatch<AppDispatch>();

const handleSubmit = () => {
  dispatch(addReview({ id: book.id, name, content }));
  dispatch(fetchBookDetails(book.id));
};

//...
<Button onClick={handleSubmit}>Submit</Button>
//...
```

The useDispatch hook is used to access the Redux store's dispatch function. When the submit button is clicked (onClick event), the addReview action is dispatched with the book ID, name, and content. Additionally, the fetchBookDetails action is dispatched to retrieve the updated book details.

Then we can use the afterEach to do all of the cleanup, just like before:

```
afterEach(() => {
  cy.request('DELETE', 'http://localhost:8080/books/1/reviews');
})
```

And surely we need to define a new endpoint in our stub server:

```
server.delete('/books/:id/reviews', (req, res) => {
  const { id } = req.params;

  const book = router.db.get('books').find({ id:
  parseInt(id) }).value();
  book.reviews = [];
  router.db.write();

  res.sendStatus(204);
});
```

It deletes all reviews associated with a specific book by setting the reviews property of the book to an empty array. Now we don't have to worry about a single failing test causing issues for another test.

Refactoring

We have now finished implementing the Review creation and retrieval. Our test coverage remains high, which is great. With those tests in place, we can refactor confidently and fearlessly. For the BookDetail component, the form is self-contained and should have its own file:

```
const ReviewForm = ({ book }: { book: Book }) => {
  const [name, setName] = useState<string>("");
  const [content, setContent] = useState<string>("");
  const dispatch = useDispatch<AppDispatch>();

  const handleSubmit = () => {
    dispatch(addReview({ id: book.id, name, content }));
    dispatch(fetchBookDetails(book.id));
  };

  return (
    <form noValidate autoComplete="off">
      <TextField
        data-testid="name"
        value={name}
        onChange={(e) => setName(e.target.value)}
      />

      <TextField
        data-testid="content"
        value={content}
        onChange={(e) => setContent(e.target.value)}
      />
```

```
      <Button
        data-testid="submit"
        onClick={() => handleSubmit()}
      >
        Submit
      </Button>
    </form>
  );
};

export default ReviewForm;
```

Note here I have removed some cumbersome attributes for the TextField and Button. After performing the extraction, the `BookDetail` component becomes more streamlined and concise:

```
import ReviewForm from "./ReviewForm";

const BookDetail = ({ book }: { book: Book }) => {
  return (
    <div className="detail">
      <h2 className="book-title">{book.name}</h2>
      <p className="book-description" data-testid="book-
      description">
        {getDescriptionFor(book)}
      </p>
      <ReviewForm book={book} />
      {book.reviews && <ReviewList reviews={book.reviews} />}
    </div>
  );
};
```

And for the functional test in cypress, we can extract some helper functions to simplify the test case:

```
it('Write a review for a book', () => {
  gotoNthBookInTheList(0);
  checkBookDetail();
  composeReview('Juntao Qiu', 'Excellent work!');
  checkReview();
});
```

Functions composeReview and checkReview are defined as

```
const composeReview = (name: string, content:string) => {
  cy.get('input[name="name"]').type(name);
  cy.get('textarea[name="content"]').type(content);
  cy.get('button[name="submit"]').click();
};

const checkReview = () => {
  cy.get('div[data-testid="reviews-container"] .review').
    should('have.length', 1);
}
```

Add More Fields

If you take a close look at the Review, you'll find some important information missing: username and time of creation. We need to complete those fields:

```
it("renders book review detailed information", () => {
  const reviews = [
    {
      id: 1,
      bookId: 1,
```

```
      name: "Juntao Qiu",
      date: "2023/06/21",
      content: "Excellent work, really impressed by your
      efforts",
    },
  ];

  render(<ReviewList reviews={reviews} />);
  expect(screen.getByTestId("name")).toHaveTextContent
  ("Juntao Qiu");
  expect(screen.getByTestId("review-content")).toHaveText
  Content(
    "Excellent work, really impressed by your efforts"
  );
});
```

The implementation should be effortless:

```
{reviews.map((review) => (
  <div data-testid="review" className="review" key={review.id}>
    <div data-testid="name">{review.name}</div>
    <p data-testid="review-content">{review.content}</p>
  </div>
))}
```

As the code in map keeps growing, we can extract it to a separate file – Review:

```
const ReviewItem = ({review}: { review: Review }) => {
  return (
    <div data-testid="review" className="review"
    key={review.id}>
      <div data-testid="name">{review.name}</div>
      <p data-testid="review-content">{review.content}</p>
```

```
      </div>
  );
};
```

And use it as a pure presentational component:

```
import ReviewItem from "./ReviewItem";

const ReviewList = ({ reviews }: { reviews: Review[] }) => {
  return (
    <div data-testid="reviews-container">
      {reviews.map((review) => (
        <ReviewItem key={review.id} review={review} />
      ))}
    </div>
  );
};
```

Since all the logic for rendering a review has been moved to its own component, we can move the corresponding test as well:

```
describe("ReviewItem", () => {
  it("renders", () => {
    const review = {
      id: 1,
      bookId: 1,
      name: "Juntao Qiu",
      date: "2023/06/21",
      content: "Excellent work, really impressed by your
      efforts",
    };

    render(<ReviewItem review={review} />);
```

```
expect(screen.getByTestId("name")).toHaveTextContent
("Juntao Qiu");
expect(screen.getByTestId("review-content")).toHaveText
Content(
  "Excellent work, really impressed by your efforts"
);
});
})
```

By following this approach, testing different data variations becomes simpler. For instance, if there is a requirement to display the date in a relative format, such as "Posted 5 mins ago" or "Posted yesterday," instead of an absolute date, there is no need to modify the ReviewList component.

All tests have successfully passed, indicating the robustness of our code, as shown in Figure 10-3.

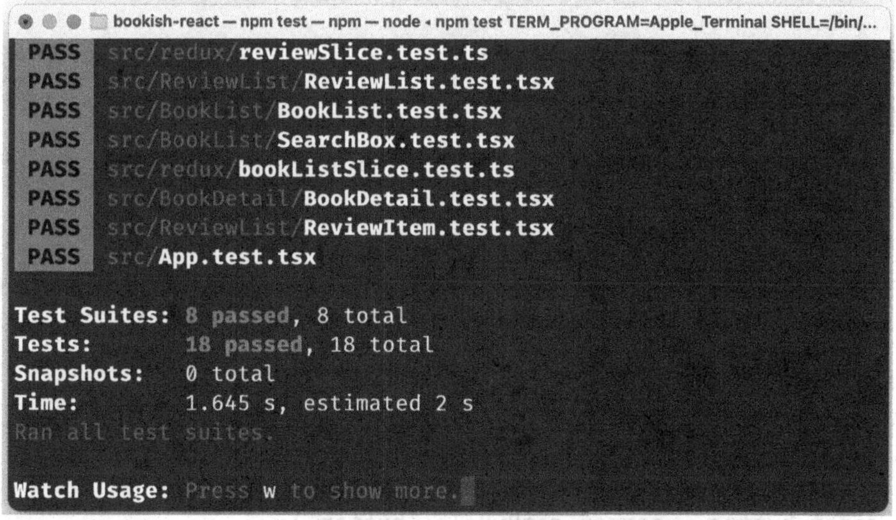

Figure 10-3. *All tests are passing after all code changes*

It is now more streamlined, with each component having a clear and well-defined purpose. The comprehensive test coverage ensures that any refactoring or modifications won't inadvertently introduce errors. We can proceed confidently, knowing that our code is both reliable and maintainable.

Review Editing

The Review component now provides basic presentation. However, in the real world, the user could have left a typo in their review or would completely rewrite the content. We need to allow the user to edit the Review they have already posted.

We need to add an Edit button that will change to a Submit button when clicked (waiting for the user to submit). When a user clicks Submit, the text turns to Edit again. So the first test could be

```
it('edit a review item', () => {
  const review = {
    id: 1,
    bookId: 1,
    name: "Juntao Qiu",
    date: "2023/06/21",
    content: "Excellent work, really impressed by your
    efforts",
  };

  render(<ReviewItem review={review} />);

  const button = screen.getByRole('button');
  expect(button).toHaveTextContent('Edit');
```

```
act(() => {
  userEvent.click(button);
})

expect(button).toHaveTextContent('Submit');
})
```

By using userEvent.click, we can simulate the click event on the Edit button and verify the text changes on the button. We can achieve that by introducing state to the component:

```
const [editing, setEditing] = useState(false);
```

All we need to do is toggle the status of editing. For rendering, we can decide which text to display by the editing state like this:

```
const ReviewItem = ({ review }: { review: Review }) => {
  const [editing, setEditing] = useState<boolean>(false);

  return (
    <div data-testid="review" className="review"
    key={review.id}>
      <div data-testid="name">{review.name}</div>
      <p data-testid="review-content">{review.content}</p>
      <Button
        onClick={() => setEditing(!editing)}
      >
        {!editing ? "Edit" : "Submit"}
      </Button>
    </div>
  );
};
```

We'd like a textarea to show up when the user clicks Edit and copy all the review content into the textarea for editing:

```
it("copy content to a textarea for editing", () => {
  const review = {
    id: 1,
    bookId: 1,
    name: "Juntao Qiu",
    date: "2023/06/21",
    content: "Excellent work, really impressed by your efforts",
  };

  render(<ReviewItem review={review} />);

  const button = screen.getByRole("button");
  const content = screen.getByTestId("review-content");

  expect(content).toBeInTheDocument();

  act(() => {
    userEvent.click(button);
  });

  const editingContent = screen.getByRole("textbox");
  expect(content).not.toBeInTheDocument();

  expect(editingContent).toBeInTheDocument();
  expect(editingContent).toHaveValue(
    "Excellent work, really impressed by your efforts"
  );
});
```

To implement that, we have to maintain that content in state as well:

```
const [content, setContent] = useState<string>(review.content);
```

And render the textarea and static text based on the editing state:

```
{!editing ? (
  <p data-testid="review-content">{review.content}</p>
) : (
  <TextField
    name="content"
    label="Content"
    margin="normal"
    variant="outlined"
    multiline
    value={content}
    onChange={(e) => setContent(e.target.value)}
  />
)}
```

The Review component now has two distinct states: "viewing" and "editing," which can be toggled by clicking the "edit" button. In order to persist the updated content to the backend, we need to define an action.

Save a Review – Action and Reducer

Just like the process for creating a review, to save a review we need to send a request to the backend. The good news is that json-server already provides this functionality. We send a PUT request to http://localhost:8080/books/<book-id>/reviews/<id> to update a review.

With RESTful style API, when you update some existing resource, you use PUT as the HTTP verb. Let's update reviewSlice.ts with a new async action:

```
type UpdateReviewRequest = {
  bookId: number;
  reviewId: number;
```

```
  content: string;
};

export const updateReview = createAsyncThunk<Review,
UpdateReviewRequest>(
  "reviews/updateReview",
  async ({ bookId, reviewId, content }:
  UpdateReviewRequest) => {
    try {
      const response = await axios.put(
        `http://localhost:8080/books/${bookId}/reviews/$
        {reviewId}`,
        { name, content }
      );
      return response.data;
    } catch (error) {
      throw error;
    }
  }
);
```

Correspondingly, we could have two different unit tests for the update action:

```
it("updates a review", async () => {
  const mockStore = configureStore({
    reducer: {
      reviewSliceReducer,
    },
  });
```

```
const review = {
  id: 1,
  content: "Good work",
};
const putSpy = jest.spyOn(axios, "put").mockResolvedValue
({ data: review });

await mockStore
  .dispatch(
    updateReview({
      bookId: 1,
      reviewId: 1,
      content: "Good work",
    })
  )
  .then((response) => {
    expect(response.payload).toEqual(review);
  });

expect(putSpy).toHaveBeenCalledWith(
  "http://localhost:8080/books/1/reviews/1",
  {
    content: "Good work",
  }
);
});
```

The code snippet tests the "updates review" scenario. It creates a mock store, spies on the axios.put function to track its calls, and dispatches the updateReview action. The test asserts that the action resolves with the expected payload and verifies that axios.put is called with the correct parameters.

jest.spyOn is a Jest utility function used to create a mock or spy on a function. It allows you to track the calls made to the function and define custom behaviors for the function. In the code snippet, jest. spyOn(axios, "put") is used to spy on the axios.put function, which enables us to monitor its usage and control its behavior in the test.

By using jest.spyOn, we can assert that axios.put is called with the expected parameters and provide a resolved value for the function using mockResolvedValue. This allows us to simulate a successful response from the server when testing the async action.

And for error handling cases, we'll make sure the spy is simulating a rejection:

```
it("handles network error", async () => {
  const mockStore = configureStore({
    reducer: {
      reviewSliceReducer,
    },
  });

  const error = new Error("Network error");
  const putSpy = jest.spyOn(axios, "put").mockRejectedValueOnce
  (error);

  await mockStore
    .dispatch(
      updateReview({
        bookId: 1,
        reviewId: 1,
        content: "Good work",
      })
    )
```

```
    .then((response) => {
      expect(response.type).toEqual("reviews/updateReview/
      rejected");
    });

  expect(putSpy).toHaveBeenCalledWith(
    "http://localhost:8080/books/1/reviews/1",
    {
      content: "Good work",
    }
  );
});
```

The error simulation part of the code uses `jest.spyOn` to create a spy on the `axios.put` function. By using `mockRejectedValueOnce`, it sets up the spy to return a rejected promise with the specified error object when the `axios.put` function is called during the test. This allows us to simulate a network error and test how the code handles it.

Integration All Together

Since all the parts for editing a review are ready, it's time to put them together. We need to make sure that when Submit is clicked, the remote service is called:

```
it("update the content", () => {
  const review = {
    id: 1,
    bookId: 1,
    name: "Juntao Qiu",
    date: "2023/06/21",
    content: "Excellent work, really impressed by your efforts",
  };
```

```
renderWithProvider(<ReviewItem review={review} />);

const putSpy = jest.spyOn(axios, "put").mockResolvedValue({
data: review });
const button = screen.getByRole("button");

// enter the editing mode
act(() => {
  userEvent.click(button);
});

const editingContent = screen.getByRole("textbox");
expect(editingContent).toBeInTheDocument();

act(() => {
  userEvent.clear(editingContent);
  userEvent.type(editingContent, "I mean this is fantastic");
});

// submit the form
act(() => {
  userEvent.click(button);
});

expect(putSpy).toHaveBeenCalledWith(
  "http://localhost:8080/books/1/reviews/1",
  { content: "I mean this is fantastic" }
);
});
```

The preceding code renders the ReviewItem component with
the provided review data. The axios.put function is spied on using
jest.spyOn and is set to resolve with the updated review data when called.
The test interacts with the component by clicking a button to enter
editing mode, clearing the existing content, and typing new content.

Then, another button is clicked to submit the form. The test asserts that the axios.put function was called with the correct URL and updated content.

For the user interaction, the userEvent.clear function is used to clear the existing content from the textbox, and userEvent.type is used to simulate typing the new content. After making the changes, another button is clicked to submit the form and update the review. By simulating these user interactions, the test ensures that the component is calling the appropriate API endpoint.

For the ReviewItem component, we can implement it pretty straightforwardly:

```
//...
const dispatch = useDispatch<AppDispatch>();

const updateReviewContent = () => {
  if (editing) {
    dispatch(
      updateReview({ reviewId: review.id, bookId: review.
      bookId, content })
    );
  }
  setEditing((editing) => !editing);
};

//...
    <Button
      variant="contained"
      color="primary"
      name="submit"
      onClick={updateReviewContent}
    >
      {!editing ? "Edit" : "Submit"}
    </Button>
```

Summary

In this chapter, we focused on implementing the functionality to create and update reviews for books. We made the necessary changes in the backend using json-server to support these operations, allowing us to create and update reviews under a specific book.

On the frontend side, we added the reviewSlice to our Redux store, which contains the necessary actions and reducers for handling review-related state. We also updated our components to interact with the reviewSlice, allowing users to add and update reviews.

To ensure the correctness of our implementation, we discussed various testing techniques. We covered how to test actions and reducers using Redux Toolkit's createAsyncThunk and jest.spyOn to simulate network requests and mock axios. We also explored how to test user interactions by simulating events and user input using the React Testing Library and userEvent.

By the end of this chapter, we have successfully implemented the ability to create and update reviews for books. We have also gained an understanding of how to effectively test our code to ensure its correctness and maintainability.

CHAPTER 11

Behavior-Driven Development

Behavior-Driven Development (BDD) methodology was coined by Dan North. His goal was to improve communication between business and technical teams to aid in the creation of software with business value. Miscommunication between business and technical teams is often the biggest bottleneck in the delivery of software projects, and developers often misunderstand the business goals, and business teams fail to grasp the capabilities of the technical team.

> *BDD is a process designed to aid the management and the delivery of software development projects by improving communication between engineers and business professionals. In so doing, BDD ensures all development projects remain focused on delivering what the business actually needs while meeting all requirements of the user.*
>
> —Konstantin Kudryashov, Alistair Stead, and Dan North
> from the blog post *The Beginner's Guide to BDD*

The concept evolved from established agile practices, and there are different practices used to implement BDD, but at its core it's about writing our automated tests in a human-readable language, in a way that the goal of each test can be easily understood by both the business and development teams. This encourages collaboration across roles to create

© Juntao Qiu 2023
J. Qiu, *Test-Driven Development with React and TypeScript*,
https://doi.org/10.1007/978-1-4842-9648-6_11

a shared understanding of the problem they are trying to solve and results in system documentation that is automatically tested against actual system behavior.

Some of the practices used when undertaking BDD you might have heard of include *Specification by Example* and *Living Documentation*. These practices provide specific techniques that can improve collaboration among different roles in a team. They can aid developers in understanding business goals and help them to make better decisions regarding business restrictions. `Live Document` can make sure the software behaves as expected when changes are implemented due to an update in business requirements. It aims to prevent a situation where all tests are passing, but the behavior of the system isn't correct.

When implementing BDD in your team, there are numerous tools available, and we will be showcasing one of them here: Cucumber. Cucumber is a potent tool that utilizes a Domain-Specific Language (DSL) for developers to create a human-readable document, which then produces executable code as a side effect through some clever magic that we'll discuss later.

Cucumber can be used as a communication tool between business analysts and developers who translate business rules into code. As miscommunications often lead to bugs, having a dedicated tool for this process is highly beneficial. While the Live Document generated by Cucumber may not always be executable or too costly to run regularly, it remains an excellent guide during the QA process for conducting manual tests.

Play with Cucumber

Given our existing familiarity with Cypress, it would be advantageous to utilize that knowledge in conjunction with Cucumber. The excellent news is that there exists a superb Cucumber plugin for Cypress, allowing us to utilize the two tools in tandem.

Install and Config **cucumber** Plugin

It only requires a few steps to configure and get them working together properly:

```
npm install @badeball/cypress-cucumber-preprocessor \
  @bahmutov/cypress-esbuild-preprocessor esbuild --save-dev
```

And in the Cypress configuration file `cypress.config.ts`, we need to tell Cypress to take the `feature` file as input and invoke the preprocessor to parse and execute them:

```
import { defineConfig } from "cypress";

import createBundler from "@bahmutov/cypress-esbuild-
preprocessor";
import { addCucumberPreprocessorPlugin } from "@badeball/
cypress-cucumber-preprocessor";
import createEsbuildPlugin from "@badeball/cypress-cucumber-
preprocessor/esbuild";

export default defineConfig({
  e2e: {
    specPattern: "cypress/e2e/**/*.feature",
    async setupNodeEvents(
      on: Cypress.PluginEvents,
      config: Cypress.PluginConfigOptions
    ): Promise<Cypress.PluginConfigOptions> {
      await addCucumberPreprocessorPlugin(on, config);

      on(
        "file:preprocessor",
        createBundler({
          plugins: [createEsbuildPlugin(config)],
        })
      );
```

```
      return config;
    },
  },
});
```

The code exports a default configuration for Cypress, specifically for running end-to-end (e2e) tests with Cucumber. The configuration includes the following:

- The specPattern property defines the pattern for locating feature files. It uses a glob pattern to match all .feature files in the cypress/e2e/ directory and its subdirectories.

- The setupNodeEvents function is an asynchronous function that sets up additional Node events for Cypress. It takes two parameters: on and config.

- Inside the setupNodeEvents function, the addCucumberPreprocessorPlugin function is called to add a Cucumber preprocessor plugin to Cypress. This plugin ensures proper preprocessing and parsing of feature files.

- The file:preprocessor event is configured using the createBundler function and an object with a list of plugins. The createEsbuildPlugin is one such plugin, likely responsible for transpiling or bundling the test files using the Esbuild plugin.

- The modified configuration is then returned.

And the last thing we need to modify is the TypeScript configuration tsconfig.json; (check the codebase hosted in https://github.com/Apress/Test-Driven-Development-with-React-second-edition-by-Juntao-Qiu) we need to make sure the target is **ES2017** and nodeResolution is node16. The "target": "ES2017" means the generated JavaScript code will be compatible with ECMAScript 2017. In "moduleResolution": "node16", the value "node16" indicates that the compiler will use a Node.js-style module resolution algorithm, specifically targeting Node.js version 16 and its module resolution behavior.

Live Document with cucumber

File Structure

By default, cypress-cucumber-preprocessor is looking for feature files under the cypress/e2e folder:

```
cypress
├── e2e
│   ├── bookish.feature
│   ├── bookish.spec.cy.ts
│   ├── bookish.ts
│   └── helpers.ts
```

So at runtime, cypress-cucumber-preprocessor will load *.feature and try to execute them.

The First Feature Specification

Because you can describe your test in plain English, it should be straightforward to translate the acceptance criteria we described in Chapter 3 into the format cucumber wants:

```
Feature: Book List
  As a reader
  I want to see books that are trending
  So I know what to read next
```

```
Scenario: Heading
  Given I am a bookish user
  When I open the list page
  Then I can see the title "Bookish" is listed
```

Please take note of the indentation and specific keywords used in the provided text, such as "Scenario," "Given," "When," and "Then." Certain parts of the text, such as the section beginning with "As a , I want to , So that ," are intended for human readers and not interpreted by the Cucumber framework. This section can be seen as comments in other programming languages and will not be recognized by Cucumber. The actual execution by Cucumber starts from the "Scenario" section onward.

Define the Steps

The sentences within a Scenario section are referred to as step definitions and must be translated into executable code in the background. Cucumber utilizes regular expressions to match these sentences and extract any parameters, which are then passed into the corresponding step function for execution.

Let's firstly move some helper function we used in the current end-to-end tests into a helpers.ts:

```
export const gotoApp = () => {
  cy.visit("http://localhost:3000/");
};

export const checkAppTitle = (title: string) => {
  cy.get('h2[data-test="heading"]').contains(title);
};

//...
```

Interpret Sentences by Step Definition

We can define regular expressions with Given, When, and Then functions
from a cypress-cucumber-preprocessor and do something interesting in
those functions.

For example:

```
import { When, Then, Given } from "@badeball/cypress-cucumber-
preprocessor";
import {
  checkAppTitle,
  gotoApp,
} from "./helpers";

Given(/^I am a bookish user$/, function () {
  //...
});

When(/^I open the "([^"]*)" page$/, function (page: string) {
  gotoApp();
});

Then(/^I can see the title "([^"]*)" is showing$/, function
(title: string) {
  checkAppTitle(title);
});
```

The parameters passed into Given, When, and Then functions are
pretty similar; the first one is a regular expression, which is used to match
a sentence in .feature files. The second is a similar regular expression,
which returns a callback, which will be invoked once there is a match.
If there are some patterns in the regular expression, the value will be

extracted and passed to the callback (see the Then example). This is a simple but powerful mechanism that allows us to do some interesting work – including launching the browser and checking if particular elements are showing on the page (Figure 11-1).

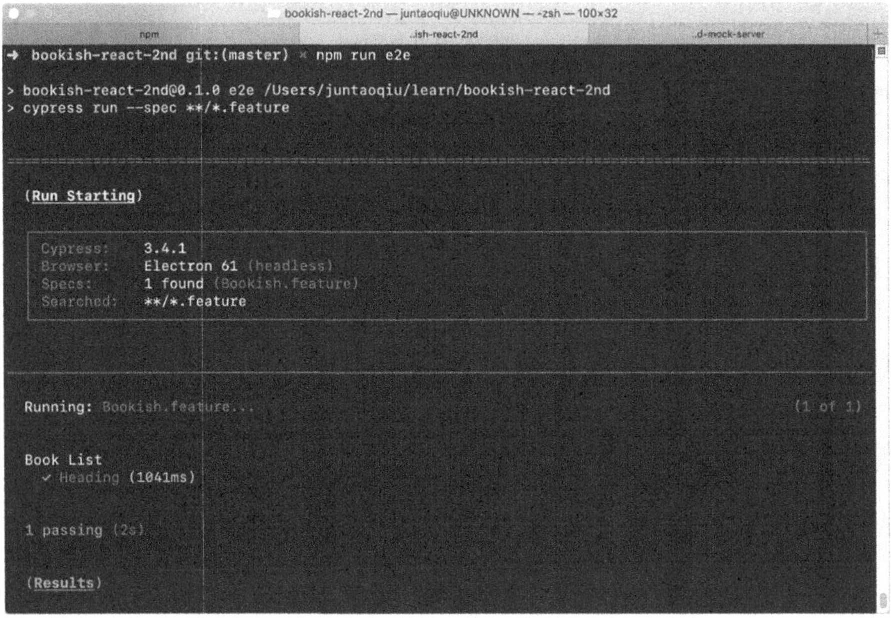

Figure 11-1. *Running cucumber with cypress in the terminal*

So, our Feature is interpreted correctly, and the parameters are extracted and passed to the method correspondingly. Note that we can reuse functions we extracted in previous chapters like gotoApp and checkAppTitle.

Book List

With every piece connected, we can now start to define a step definition with existing helper functions.

Define Book List **scenario**

```
Scenario: Book List
  Given I am a bookish user
  When I open the "list" page
  And there is a book list
    | name                                            |
    | Refactoring                                     |
    | Domain-driven design                            |
    | Building Microservices                          |
    | Acceptance Test Driven Development with React   |
```

If you have used markdown to write documentation, you will recognize the table we just defined earlier. That's right, you can define a more complex data structure in the feature file by using table: the structure enclosed by pipe |. That's a better way to organize repeatable data in your test and is both easy for reading by human beings and for parsing by code.

Use Data Table Interface

Each row will be treated as a row in a table, and you can actually define many columns for each row:

```
And there is
  | name                   | price |
  | Refactoring            | $100  |
  | Domain-driven design   | $120  |
  | Building Microservices | $80   |
```

cucumber provides a compelling DTI (Data Table Interface) to help developers to parse and use data tables. For example, if we want to get the BookList defined in the feature file within step, just use function table.rows() as shown below:

```
And(/^there is a book list$/, function (table: DataTable) {
  console.log(table.rows())
});
```

You'll see the data in the shape in your console:

```
[ [ 'Refactoring' ],
  [ 'Domain-driven design' ],
  [ 'Building Microservices' ],
  [ 'Acceptance Test Driven Development with React' ]
]
```

Alternatively, if you prefer JSON, you can call table.hashes() instead:

```
[ { name: 'Refactoring' },
  { name: 'Domain-driven design' },
  { name: 'Building Microservices' },
  { name: 'Acceptance Test Driven Development with React' } ]
```

Thus, in our step definition, we can use the DTI to do the assertion:

```
And(/^there is a book list$/, function (table: DataTable) {
  const actual = table.rows().map((row) => row[0]);
  checkBookListWith(actual);
});
```

Searching

The next scenario we can test is the searching feature. We can describe the business requirement in plain English:

```
Scenario: Search by keyword
  Given I am a bookish user
  When I open the list page
  And I typed "design" to perform a search
  Then I should see "Domain-driven design" is matched
```

Step Definitions

It is effortless to implement these steps, provided we have all the helper functions in position:

```
import { checkBookListWith, performSearch } from './helpers';

import {
  When,
  Then
} from "@badeball/cypress-cucumber-preprocessor";

When(/^I typed "([^"]*)" to perform a search$/, function
(keyword: string) {
  performSearch(keyword);
});

Then(/^I should see "([^"]*)" is matched$/, function (title:
string) {
  checkBookListWith([title]);
});
```

Neat! The step functions are almost self-explanatory. Note how we reuse existing helper functions here in step definitions.

Review Page

Similarly, we can rewrite the review feature tests in the following sentence, in English:

```
Scenario: Write a review
  Given I am a bookish user
  When I open the book detail page for the first item
  And I add a review to that book
    | name        | content        |
    | Juntao Qiu  | Excellent work! |
  Then I can see it displayed beneath the description section
  with the text "Excellent works!"
```

Again, we can reuse a lot of steps defined previously, noting that we use a Data Table Interface to extract multiple parameters passed in:

```
import {
  When,
  Then,
  Given,
  DataTable,
} from "@badeball/cypress-cucumber-preprocessor";

import {
  checkReview,
  composeReview,
  gotoApp,
  gotoNthBookInTheList
} from "./helpers";

When(/^I open the book detail page for the first item$/,
function () {
  cy.request("DELETE", "http://localhost:8080/books/1/reviews");
  gotoApp();
```

```
    gotoNthBookInTheList(0);
});

When(/^I add a review to that book$/, function (table:
DataTable) {
    const reviews = table.hashes();
    const review = reviews[0];
    composeReview(review.name, review.content);
});

Then(
    /^I can see it displayed beneath the description section with
    the text "([^"]*)"$/,
    function (content: string) {
        cy.get('div[data-testid="reviews-container"] .review')
        .should(
            "have.length",
            1
        );
        checkReview(content);
    }
);
```

By abstracting the behavior into helper functions, we can significantly improve the clarity and relevance of the text within the step function. Additionally, consolidating related code enhances the readability and maintainability of future changes. This approach enables seamless modification of specific files, such as UI elements, without impacting other sections, as it allows for easy navigation to the corresponding file.

Summary

In this chapter, we explored the concepts and benefits of Cucumber testing and Behavior-Driven Development (BDD). Cucumber is a tool that allows for the creation of executable specifications written in a language close to the business domain. We discussed how placing Cucumber tests at the end of examples improves readability, enabling stakeholders and nontechnical team members to validate system behavior easily.

One of the key advantages of Cucumber is its ability to promote collaboration between technical and nontechnical team members. By aligning tests with business objectives and using a language that closely resembles the domain, Cucumber facilitates effective communication and shared understanding of requirements.

We learned about the reusability of Cucumber tests, which reduces duplication of test code and simplifies maintenance efforts. Automation of Cucumber tests enables regression testing and faster feedback on system behavior, enhancing the overall testing process.

Finally, we discussed how Cucumber aligns with the principles of Behavior-Driven Development (BDD). By focusing on collaboration, shared understanding, and clarity in requirements, Cucumber encourages teams to work together in delivering value to stakeholders.

In conclusion, Cucumber testing and BDD provide valuable approaches to ensure the alignment of technical implementations with business requirements. By leveraging Cucumber's features, teams can enhance collaboration, improve test quality, and achieve effective communication throughout the development process.

APPENDIX A

Background of Testing Strategies

Different Layers of Tests

Different layers of tests are used in a frontend project to ensure comprehensive and reliable testing coverage. In a well-designed test suite, tests should contain at least these components: end-to-end tests, integration tests, and unit tests.

Each layer focuses on specific aspects of the application and helps identify different types of issues. Here are the key reasons for using different layers of tests:

1. *Unit tests*: Unit tests target small, isolated units of code, typically individual functions or components. They verify the behavior and functionality of these units in isolation, without dependencies on external resources. Unit tests help catch bugs early, validate edge cases, and provide quick feedback during development. They facilitate code maintainability, as changes can be made with confidence, knowing that existing functionality is preserved.

© Juntao Qiu 2023
J. Qiu, *Test-Driven Development with React and TypeScript*,
https://doi.org/10.1007/978-1-4842-9648-6

2. *Integration tests*: Integration tests verify the interactions and compatibility between various components, modules, or services within the application. They focus on testing the integration points, data flow, and communication between different parts of the system. Integration tests uncover issues that may arise when different components work together and help ensure the overall system functions correctly.

3. *End-to-end (E2E) tests*: E2E tests simulate real user interactions and scenarios, covering the entire application from start to finish. They validate the functionality and behavior of the system as a whole, including the user interface, user flows, and integrations with external services. E2E tests ensure that all components work together seamlessly and provide confidence in the overall user experience.

By incorporating these different layers of tests, the frontend project achieves a comprehensive testing strategy. Unit tests catch individual component issues, integration tests detect problems at the interaction points, and E2E tests validate the end-to-end functionality. This layered approach helps identify bugs early, promotes code quality, supports easier debugging, and builds confidence in the reliability and robustness of the frontend application.

Test Pyramid

Mike Cohn coined test pyramid in his famous book *Succeeding with Agile*, which is about how you should arrange your test structure we mentioned earlier.

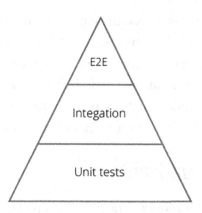

The test pyramid

Typically, you have a small number of end-to-end tests (see the top of the pyramid) and cover critical paths from the end user's perspective. And then you have a larger number of integration tests in the middle layer – those tests are making sure different components across the application can fit together and talk to each other correctly. Finally, at the bottom, you have many more unit tests that verify each building block will function well independently.

There are different ways to explain the pyramid, but the point I want to emphasize here is the higher the tests in the pyramid, the more expensive they are in terms of running cost and the less helpful they are in locating bugs.

Additionally, as you proceed further down the pyramid, the number of tests should increase, because each type of test focuses on a different perspective of the software quality. The number of tests for each type, the running time, and the feedback speed are all different from one to the next.

A long-running and fragile test suite does not help the development process, or even worse, it could deliver the wrong message to the team: `automation tests are useless`. And after some time, those test suites are seen as waste and then would be abandoned, and that could put the software system under significant risk.

The test pyramid is an excellent way for us to design and review our test strategy. If we build everything from scratch, that's easy. We just need to make sure when new tests need to be added, we always add them after reviewing the current shape of the test suites. In contrast, when we are working on a legacy system, we may need to refactor the whole test suite (if one exists) to conform to the shape of the `test pyramid` iteratively. We need to clean up the duplicated, long-running tests at the higher levels and make sure we have enough lower-level tests to support the development.

Agile Testing Quadrants

In 2003, Brian Marick introduced the Agile Testing Quadrants. It's a great tool to help the delivery team to categorize different types of tests. Later on in 2008, Lisa Crispin and Janet Gregory in their book *Agile Testing: A Practical Guide for Testers and Agile Teams* extended the concept of Agile Testing Quadrants, described in the following figure:

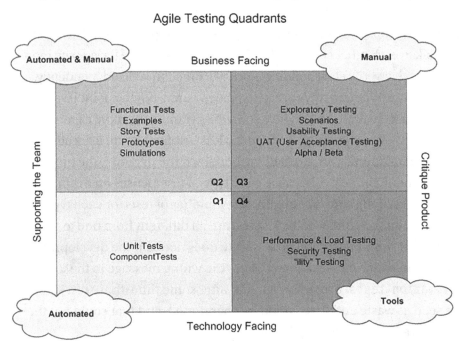

Test quadrants. Source: https://lisacrispin.com/2011/11/08/ using-the-agile-testing-quadrants/

In the preceding figure, the authors divided tests into four quadrants. Along the X axis, tests in the left-hand quadrants help the delivery team to understand **what** should be tested, and tests on the right-hand side help them to evaluate the system from the outside. For the Y axis, tests on the top ensure the code meets the business requirements, while tests at the bottom are related more to internal quality.

Since we're focusing on a `test-first` approach to understand business requirements and then drive the production code from a developer's perspective, we will only discuss tests in Q1 and Q2 in this book. In the chart, acceptance tests check if our code is meeting the business requirements, while unit tests and integration tests focus on technical details.

Compared to exploratory tests or performance tests on the right, all of those tests are used for supporting developers to write **correct** (i.e., meets the requirements) code.

Summary

Different layers of tests are utilized in frontend projects to ensure comprehensive testing coverage and reliable software quality. The concept of the test pyramid, introduced by Mike Cohn, emphasizes the importance of a balanced test structure. By employing these different layers and adopting a test-first approach, frontend projects can achieve comprehensive testing, ensure code correctness, and maintain high software quality.

APPENDIX B

A Short Introduction to TypeScript

This appendix introduces some of the key features of TypeScript used in the book. While not a comprehensive reference (as new features are continuously added to the language), it provides enough context to understand all the examples discussed in the book.

TypeScript's static type checking is an effective way to reduce potential bugs in a weakly typed language like JavaScript. Though it may take time to become familiar with all the concepts, it's worthwhile to learn and apply them in your codebase.

The Language

TypeScript is a typed superset of JavaScript that adds optional static typing and other features to the language. It allows developers to catch errors and bugs at compile time instead of runtime, making their code more robust and maintainable. TypeScript also provides advanced features like classes, interfaces, and modules that make it easier to write large-scale applications.

TypeScript code needs to be compiled before it can be executed in a browser or in a JavaScript runtime environment. When you write TypeScript code, you use TypeScript syntax and features that are not compatible with standard JavaScript engines.

© Juntao Qiu 2023
J. Qiu, *Test-Driven Development with React and TypeScript*,
https://doi.org/10.1007/978-1-4842-9648-6

The TypeScript compiler then takes your TypeScript code and compiles it into JavaScript code that can be executed in a browser or in a JavaScript runtime environment (like in Node).

Primitive Types

TypeScript provides several built-in primitive types, including number, string, boolean, and void. Use these types to declare the type of a variable or parameter in your TypeScript code. By explicitly declaring the type of a variable or parameter, you can catch errors early on and help ensure that your code is more maintainable and robust:

```
const age: number = 38;
const name: string = "Juntao Qiu";
const isDone: boolean = false;

function sayHello(): void {
  console.log("Hello!");
}
```

These built-in primitive types can be used anywhere when you need a variable, a parameter, or a return value from a function:

```
function greeting(message: string): void {
    console.log(`Hello, ${message}`);
}
```

or a helper function capitalize (takes a string as input and returns a string) can be defined as

```
function capitalize(str: string): string {
  return str.charAt(0).toUpperCase() + str.slice(1);
}
```

Custom Types

A custom type is a type that you define yourself, either by combining existing types or by creating new types from scratch. Custom types can be used to define the structure and behavior of objects in your code and can help make your code more expressive and self-documenting.

Interface

An interface is a way to describe the shape of an object or function in TypeScript. Use interfaces to create contracts between different parts of your code or when you need to define a complex type that is used in multiple places. By using interfaces, you can make your code more modular and reusable. Interfaces can help catch errors early on and make it easier to refactor your code later on.

```
interface Person {
  firstName: string;
  lastName: string;
  age: number;
}

const person: Person = {
  firstName: "Juntao",
  lastName: "Qiu",
  age: 38
};
```

You can also define methods in an interface, just like in other programming languages:

```
interface OrderItem {
  id: number;
  name: string;
```

```
  price: number;
  quantity: number;
}

interface Order {
  id: number;
  items: OrderItem[];
  totalPrice: number;
  status: "pending" | "shipped" | "delivered";
  addItem(item: OrderItem): void;
  removeItem(item: OrderItem): void;
  updateStatus(status: "pending" | "shipped" |
  "delivered"): void;
}
```

Note the status field is defined as "pending" | "shipped" | "delivered"; it's called union type, which means that a value can have one of several possible types. So you can call method updateStatus with one of these values, but other values will be rejected during the type checks.

Class

In TypeScript, a class is a blueprint for creating objects that share a common structure and behavior. Classes are used to define the properties and methods of an object and can be used to create multiple instances of that object:

```
class Product {
  constructor(public id: number, public name: string, public
  price: number) {}
}

const product = new Product(1, "Widget", 10.99);
```

For a `ShoppingCart`, you can define `private` fields in a class that can only be accessed internally with a `this.` prefix:

```typescript
class ShoppingCart {
  private items: Item[];
  constructor() {
    this.items = [];
  }

  addItem(item: Item) {
    this.items.push(item);
  }

  removeItem(item: Item) {
    const index = this.items.findIndex((i) => i.id ===
    item.id);
    if (index > -1) {
      this.items.splice(index, 1);
    }
  }

  get totalPrice() {
    return this.items.reduce((total, item) => total + item.
    price, 0);
  }
}
```

Please note the get in the `totalPrice` method indicates that it is a getter. You use a getter just like a regular property of the class instances:

```typescript
it('get the total price', () => {
  const shoppingCart = new ShoppingCart();

  shoppingCart.addItem({
    id: "1",
```

```
  name: "Test-Driven Development with React",
  price: 50.0
});

expect(shoppingCart.totalPrice).toEqual(50.0);
})
```

Type Alias

In TypeScript, a type alias is a way to create a new name for an existing type or to define a new type based on an existing type:

```
type Person = {
  name: string;
  age: number;
  email: string;
};
```

And you can use the Person like the built-in primitive types in a variable definition, function parameter, or return value:

```
const person: Person = {
  name: "Juntao",
  age: 38,
  email: "juntao.qiu@gmail.com"
};

function sendEmailToPerson(person: Person): void {
  // Send email
}

sendEmailToPerson(person);
```

Type aliases can also be used to define union types, intersection types, or other complex types. For example:

```typescript
type Status = "pending" | "shipped" | "delivered";

type Order = {
  id: number;
  items: string[];
  status: Status;
};

type EnhancedOrder = Order & {
  customerName: string;
  totalPrice: number;
};
```

In the preceding code, we define three type aliases: Status, Order, and EnhancedOrder. The Status type alias defines a union type of string literals that represent the possible values for the status property in the Order type. The Order type alias defines an object with three properties: id, items, and status, where the status property must be one of the possible values defined in the Status type alias. Finally, the EnhancedOrder type alias **extends** the Order type with two additional properties: customerName and totalPrice.

The & symbol is used to create an intersection type, which represents a type that has all the properties of two or more types. An intersection type is formed by combining two or more types with the & operator.

Summary

In summary, using TypeScript with React can provide developers with a range of benefits. TypeScript allows you to specify types for your React components, props, and state, providing improved type safety and catching errors early on. It can also make your code more self-documenting and expressive and help organize your code more effectively. Additionally, TypeScript can make it easier to refactor your code by identifying all the places where a certain type or interface is used.

By using TypeScript, you can write more robust and maintainable code that is easier to scale and collaborate on with other developers.

Index

A

Acceptance test, 4, 153
Acceptance Test–Driven
    Development (ATDD), 5, 6,
    81, 167, 198
add function, 20, 70
Advertising management
    system, 197
axios.put function, 225–228

B

beforeAll and afterAll functions, 25
Behavior-driven development
    (BDD), 8
    Cucumber, 232–234
      book list, 238–240
      feature specification, 235, 236
      file structure, 235
      review page, 242, 243
      searching, 240, 241
      step function, 236–238
    developers, 232
    miscommunication, 231
Book detail view
    acceptance tests
      detail page, 126
      functionality, 125

default value, 146, 147, 149
frontend routing
    BookDetailContainer, 132
    BookDetailContainer.tsx,
      129, 130
    index.tsx, 128, 129
    react-router, 127
    useBook hook, 131
length of description,
    149, 150
testing data, 141, 142
unit tests
    book detail page, 137, 138
    file structure, 139–141
    refactoring, 133–136
user interface
    refinement, 143–145
Book list
    acceptance test
      add list, 97, 98
      extract component,
        103, 104
      extract function, 101, 102
      verify book name, 99
    backend server
      async request, 108, 109
      setup/teardown, 110–113
      stub, 105–107

© Juntao Qiu 2023
J. Qiu, *Test-Driven Development with React and TypeScript*,
https://doi.org/10.1007/978-1-4842-9648-6

Book list (*cont.*)
    loading indicator
        network connection, 114
        react hooks, 118–120
        refactor first, 114–118
    unit tests, 120–123
BookListContainer, 116–118
Book reviews
    add more fields, 216–219
    business requirements
        BookDetail, 201, 202
        BookDetail
          component, 203–205
        empty list, 198, 199
        static data, 200
    end-to-end test
        cypress test, 206
        detail page, 206
        refactoring, 214–216
        review slice, 207–209
        stub server, 209–214
    review editing
        edit, 220–223
        integration, 227, 228
        save a review, 223–226
Building Microservices, 112, 113,
    142, 164–166

C

createAsyncThunk function, 181
create-react-app package, 84
Create, Read, Update, Delete
    (CRUD), 106, 198

createSlice function, 169
Cucumber, 232, 244
Cypress, 167
Cypress end-to-end UI testing
    framework, 81

D

describe function, 19
Domain-driven design, 110, 112, 154
Domain-Specific Language
    (DSL), 8, 232

E, F

End-to-end (E2E) tests, 246

G

Given-When-Then (GWT), 66

H

Helper function, 236

I

Integration tests, 189, 246

J, K, L

JavaScript testing framework, 15
Jest
    calc.test.ts, 18
    example, 21

file name patterns, 19

function add, 20

matchers

    array/object, 27, 28

    equality, 25

    expect.extend, 32, 33

    expect object, 28–30

    jsonpath, 31, 32

    .not, 26, 27

mocking/stubbing

    implementation, 35

    jest.fn, 35

    remote service call, 36

setup environment, 15–18

setup/tear down, 23, 25

test maintainer friendly, 22

jest.fn(), 160

jest.spyOn, 226

Jest testing framework, 12

M, N, O

Material UI, 81, 151

MVVM libraries, 170

P, Q

Project setup

    application requirements, 81–84

    create-react-app package,
        84, 86, 87

    install Cypress

        async/await, 91

        end-to-end test, 93, 94

        setup, 91, 92

        shortcut command, 94, 95

        version control, 95

    Material UI, 88–90

Publish-Subscribe (Pub-Sub)
    pattern, 171

R

React function, 61

React hooks, 118

react-router, 127, 128

React Testing Library, 135, 230

Red-Green-Refactor, 2, 4

Redux, 169, 172

Refactoring, 124

    arrow function, 61

    code smells

        Big Props List, 41

        design principles, 44

        long files, 40

        mixing computation,
            views, 42

        mocks, 43, 44

        projects, 40

    extract constant, 49, 58

    extract function, 50, 53, 54, 56

    extract parameter, 57

    if-else, 55

    implementation, 45–47

    mastering, 39

    moce fields, 60

    rename parameter, 51

    rename variable, 52

Refactoring (*cont.*)
    simplify logic, 62
    slide statements, 48, 59
Refactoring techniques, 65
render method, 100, 122
ReviewList component, 202, 205

S

SearchBox, 158, 159
Search functionality
    acceptance test
        BookListContainer, 157
        book title, 158
        components, 162, 163
        hook, 156
        requirement, 160
        SearchBox, 158–161
        test code, 163–166
        TextField, 154
        useBooks, 155
        useEffect hook, 155
    discovery process, 153
    useBooks, 156
setupNodeEvents function, 234
Slice, 179, 197
spacing property, 145
specPattern property, 234
State management
    build UI, 170, 171
    decoupling data/view,
        174, 175
    formula view = f(state), 177

    implementation
        environment setup, 178
        fetching data from
            remote, 181–183
        slice, 179
        store, 183–185
    library, 193, 194
    migrate application
        book details slice, 190–192
        book list container, 186, 187
        Redux, 185
        SearchBox
            component, 187–189
        test individual reducers,
            189, 190
    pub-sub pattern, 171, 172
    Redux, 172, 173
Step functions, 241
Stub server, 106

T

Test-Driven Development (TDD)
    ATDD, 6, 7
    BDD, 8
    first test, 75
    Mark d, 75
    Notes d and D, 76
    practical approaches, 1
    prerequisites, 8, 9
    Red-Green-Refactor, 2–4
    refactoring, 77–79
    tasking, 10, 11

parser, tracking
  progress, 73, 74
  subtasks, 72
  system, 73
techniques, 10
tests, 1
types, 5
writing test, 65, 66, 68
Testing strategies
agile testing quadrants,
  248, 249
E2E tests, 246
integration, 246
unit tests, 245
test pyramid, 247
totalPrice method, 255
translate function, 77
Triangulation method
function addition, 69–71
writing test, 69

TypeScript
custom type
  class, 254, 255
  definition, 253
  interface, 253, 254
  react components, 258
  type alias, 256, 257
definition, 251
features, 251
primitive types, 252
static type checking, 251

U, V, W, X

Unit tests, 245–247, 249
userEvent.clear function, 229

Y, Z

YAGNI, 5

Printed in the United States
by Baker & Taylor Publisher Services